D1055343

Being, Nothingness, and Fly Fishing

BOOKS BY MICHAEL CHECCHIO

A Clean, Well-Lighted Stream

*Sundown Legends: A Journey into the
American Southwest*

Being, Nothingness, and Fly Fishing

Being, Nothingness, and Fly Fishing

MICHAEL CHECCHIO

The Lyons Press

Guilford, Connecticut

An imprint of The Globe Pequot Press

The Lyons Press is an imprint of The Globe Pequot Press.

Portions of this book were published in somewhat different form as essays in the following periodicals: *Gray's Sporting Journal, California Fly Fisher, Trout, In-Fisherman, Trout/Salmon/Steelheader,* and *San Francisco Focus.*

Printed in the United States of America

10 9 8 7 6 5 4 3 2 1

Design by Compset

Library of Congress Cataloging-in-Publication Data is available on file.

ISBN 1-58574-341-0

Contents

INTRODUCTION

I've been fly fishing for trout for a little more than twenty years. But I think maybe the time has come for me to give it up. At least for a little while. My decision is neither as dramatic nor as drastic as it sounds.

This past summer I was fly fishing for steelhead on the North Umpqua River in Oregon. The steelhead were late coming into the famous fly-fishing stretch of the canyon on the North Fork. The main run of summer steelhead can usually be counted on to show up in the Camp Water by the second or third week of July. But not this season. No one quite understood what was going on. I doubted that more than a hundred steelhead were scattered throughout the thirty or so miles of river canyon. Things were so slow that very few anglers had even bothered to show up. The upshot of this was that I had the river pretty much to myself.

I spied a familiar, beat-up green Chevy pickup parked at a turnout above the north bank. I wasn't surprised to see Lee Spencer there. Lee is well known on the river. A sticker pasted on his truck's bumper reads: BACK TO THE PLEISTOCENE. Plastic dinosaurs are plastered all over the dashboard. A toy turtle hangs from the rearview mirror.

Lee's an archaeologist by profession, a fly fisherman by temperament. He begins every summer season fishing on the North Umpqua well before anyone else, in May, arriving even before the summer run of steelhead. And he fishes every day of the summer run, right through the end of October. He favors a two-handed Spey rod, and he fishes dry flies exclusively. He told me that the previous season he had landed seventy-six steelhead—all on dry flies.

I met up with Lee down by the river. He showed me the flies he was using this season. He had taken a pair of wire cutters and deliberately removed the points from each one of his hooks. Lee told me that he'd accidentally killed two wild fish the previous season, and he was beginning to reexamine the ethics of his sport. His solution was to break off the hook points. He didn't want to hurt the fish, but he didn't want to give up fishing altogether, either. Lee was satisfied with just getting a single jump or a pull from a steelhead before it slipped free from his broken hook. Just

2

feeling that momentary electric jolt of life on the end of his line was enough for him.

"I'm not saying that this is for the whole world," Lee told me. "It's just a place where I'm at right now."

I wasn't certain if I was ready for Lee's brand of fishing Taoism just yet. Perhaps someday when I evolve more fully as a human being, I'll be ready to remove the points from my hooks, too.

I've been fortunate enough to have fished for trout on something like sixty-three American rivers. The great majority of those streams were located in the West. That's not an immodest number, given the fact that I've been fly fishing for a little over twenty years. But it's more than enough trout fishing for me at the moment.

I find that of all the rivers on which I've fished for trout, the only two I have any real desire to return to and fish again are the Firehole and the Henry's Fork. As Lee would put it, it's just a place where I'm at right now. The Firehole and the Henry's Fork are the two trout rivers that mean the most to me. And not coincidentally, they are the two most beautiful, in my humble opinion.

Meanwhile, as I write this, I'm getting ready to leave on a steelhead trip to British Columbia. It occurs to me that while I have fished a sufficient number of trout rivers to make me reasonably happy and content, I haven't fished nearly as many steelhead rivers as I'd like. And I have never once fished for Atlantic salmon, an omission I plan to do something about. I have a feeling I have to catch up with something I've missed out on. And so I plan to spend the remainder of my middle age fishing for salmon and steelhead.

I find that's pretty much what I've been doing anyway. Lately I've found that when I go out for sport, it's for salmon and steelhead, and never for trout anymore. Why, I can't remember the last time I went trout fishing. (Well, actually I can; it was two summers ago in New Mexico. I was researching a book about the American desert Southwest. I brought a fly rod along, just in case. I ended up fishing the San Juan, Chama, Brazos, and Cimarron rivers, all for the first time. Now, I don't think I would have made a special trip to New Mexico just to go trout fishing. But since I was going to be in the northern highlands of New Mexico anyway, I figured it would be foolish not to take advantage of the situation.)

Salmon and steelhead leave me very little time for trout these days. I don't know . . . there's just something about those fish, something heroic in the journey and life cycle of salmon and steelhead, something about the challenges involved in catching one, something about the size of the fish, and the battle. For one thing, it's trout fishing stripped of all its prissiness.

Maybe I'll go back to trout fishing when I'm too old to handle anything tougher than a spring creek or the Old Mill Pond. Trout are beautiful, but salmon and steelhead fill me with a near religious wonder.

I don't use the term *religious* lightly. Asked what his religion might be, the great West Coast landscape painter Gottardo Piazonni is said to have replied, "I think it's California." His grandson Russell Chatham—a painter, writer, and fly fisherman—once filled out an author's questionnaire by writing in the space marked RELIGION: "salmon fishing." I think I know what grandfather and grandson were getting at.

Geoffrey Norman wrote: "Fishing as a method to find comfort, or at least to escape from pain, is a reliable notion, even a cliché. But that makes it no less true. You are alone, yet you are also involved. While the activity puts some distance between you and the world, it also absorbs you so thoroughly into another, mysterious universe that you simply forget. This is something all anglers know, and it probably explains why fishing is, for so many, an alternative to church or therapy."

Thomas McGuane summed it this way: "The motto of every serious angler is, 'Nearer my God to Thee.'"

And yet while I use the term *religious* quite seriously, I do so as a totally unreligious person. Several years ago Alex Beam wrote a column for the *Boston Globe* mocking meditative fly-fishing books. The columnist found each book more pitiable and narcissistic than the last. Beam noted that "once the boys get that rod in their hands, things get real spiritual real fast." He even had some advice for authors seeking an advance from a publishing house. Beam suggested a working title for the manuscript: "Being,

Nothingness, and Fly Fishing." Fly fishermen were pissed, but I thought that was pretty funny.

And so I'm taking Beam's advice, albeit ironically. Fly fishing may be seen as a way of existing meaningfully in our time. As much as that is possible, which is never much. We come out of nothing, we go back into nothing—but we have the evening rise on the Henry's Fork. The world is all we get, and that should be enough for anyone. Each of us has had the staggering good luck to be born. And we live in a world where there is fishing. It's one of the oldest themes: We seek in nature a consolation for our mortality.

Fishing is only one means of perceiving the majesty of our planetary world. And no greater majesty can be available to the human senses. Neither our perception nor our imagination can create a world beyond or a world to come with the sublimity and rapture of earthly life. Perhaps in the end, fly fishermen try to make a kind of healing connection with the world. Fishing lifts us above the ordinary, all the while keeping us connected to simple things.

And so in a few days I'll be in the wilds of British Columbia searching for a steelhead Valhalla. I'm looking forward to my trip. This will be my first time in British Columbia. I hope to fish such rivers as the Bulkley, the Babine, the Sustut, and other famous streams in the Skeena drainage. I expect to spend an entire month up there. I have a contract to write a book about the experience. Nice work if you can get it.

As for fishing salmon and steelhead exclusively from now on, I think there are stages in a fisherman's life. I have come to a certain stage in mine. Samuel Johnson once remarked: "Claret is the liquor for boys; port the wine for men; but he who aspires to be a hero must drink brandy." And so I'm going to be a hero. (Johnson also defined the sport of angling as a worm on one end of a line and a fool on the other. Something to keep in mind.)

I suppose that after more than twenty years of fly fishing, I've come to acquire a few prejudices about the sport. And because I enjoy this kind of thing, and because I suspect you do also, I'd like to share some of my biases.

Despite the amount of time I've spent fly fishing on the Henry's Fork on the Railroad Ranch, I have never once been present for the famous green drake hatch. The idea of so many fly fishermen crowding a river at one time spoils the experience for me. Likewise I have never fished the famous salmonfly hatch on the Madison River, where as many as a hundred boats and rafts drift downriver from McAtee Bridge in a single day. No thanks. For these same reasons I have never fished the Bighorn in Montana. I understand the crowds are so bad on the Bighorn that fist fights have broken out. Now, I enjoy a fist fight as much as the next fellow, but in a bar, not on a trout stream.

With that said, I must admit that I have participated in any number of opening days on the Yellowstone River, casting shoulder to shoulder with crowds of fly fishermen at Buffalo Ford in

Yellowstone National Park. And so what if I contradict myself? Like Walt Whitman, I contain multitudes.

If you were to ask me to rate the trout fishing in the Rocky Mountain West, I would say that Wyoming has the best. This is mostly because of Yellowstone Park. When you add the scenery on the Snake River under the Grand Tetons, I think this tips the balance in the state's favor. Wyoming also has the advantage of having the Firehole River. There is no trout stream that gives me greater pleasure to fish or simply look at. And it's the river on which I really trained myself to become a fly fisherman.

Now this might surprise many, but I rank the fishing in Idaho above that in Montana. And to me it's not even a close call. I know what you're thinking—Montana is the Mecca of American trout fishing, the last best place, and all that malarkey. But Idaho has the Henry's Fork of the Snake River. And the dry-fly fishing on the gigantic meadow stream on the Railroad Ranch transcends the ordinary to become archetype. Idaho also has what might rightly be considered the finest spring creek in the West—Silver Creek. And it's got something else that Montana doesn't have—steelhead, in the Snake, the Salmon, and the Clearwater rivers.

As for Montana, my favorite river is the Yellowstone. I love this river where it passes in braided channels by Mallard's Rest under the Abasaroka Mountains south of Livingston. This spangled blue water is best fished in autumn under golden cottonwood trees. The Absarokas are in some ways even more interesting to look at than the Tetons, although they aren't quite as big or dramatic.

For the past decade I have made my home in San Francisco. So I've had many opportunities to fish for trout in California. And I can state flatly that there isn't a single trout river in California that can compare with the best of those trout streams in Wyoming, Idaho, or Montana. The McCloud in its timbered canyon would be my choice for California's premier blue-ribbon trout stream. It wouldn't even make my top-ten list in Montana. I would rank Hat Creek as California's premier spring creek, although it's a poor man's Silver Creek. Now, many California fly fishermen would say I don't know what the hell I'm talking about, that Fall River is California's best spring creek. But you need a boat to fish Fall River, and for me, wading a trout stream and feeling the current against my legs is half the pleasure in fly fishing.

Now we come to the Sierra Nevada. The views are priceless. This is one of the most impressive backdrops on earth for wetting a line. And I've landed brown trout on the East Walker River near the Nevada border that were as large as any trout I've ever caught in Montana. But Sierra rivers draw big crowds, especially from southern California.

If you were to ask me (and I realize nobody has) to rate California's trout fishing overall, I'd give it a grade of B minus. And for godsakes, don't write or call me to argue or complain. I especially don't want to hear from any pissed-off fishing guides or lodge owners. It doesn't matter what I think about your favorite trout streams anyway; what's important is what you think about them.

I find California's trout fishing to be generally mediocre, but I stay for the salmon and steelhead fishing. The West Coast is the only place in the United States where you can fish for steelhead in their native habitat. If it weren't for salmon and steelhead, I doubt very much that I'd be living in California.

I am painfully aware that California's once matchless steelhead rivers have been irreparably damaged by dam building. Too many river miles are drowned under artificial lakes and impoundments. And I haven't even mentioned the murderous logging programs. But one California river very near the Oregon border stands apart from this tragedy. Not only does the river host some of the largest king salmon and steelhead on the West Coast during autumn and winter, but it's also unmatched for its pristine clarity, wildness, and visual splendor. Not coincidentally, it's the last major un-dammed river in California. I am of course speaking about the Smith River in the majestic redwood country.

The only problem with the Smith is that it gets terribly crowded when the salmon and steelhead are running. But there are ways to get around the many fishermen and driftboats. I avoid the main-stem Smith when the fishing becomes too sociable, by hiking down into the rugged canyon of its South Fork. The South Fork is the wildest and most scenic part of the Smith; the place least likely to hold another angler; and the place most likely to surrender a trophy steelhead. (Normally I wouldn't mention any of this, but the South Fork was recently exposed in a fly-fishing magazine.)

But the best thing about living where I do in California is that I'm only an eight-hour drive away from what is undoubtedly the finest and most beautiful summer steelhead river in the United States: the North Umpqua River in Oregon. I can leave my home at a reasonable hour in the morning and by late afternoon be fishing on the famous Camp Water.

I've gotten to know the North Umpqua better than any other river I've fished, even the Firehole. I don't mean to sound melodramatic, but I think the Umpqua, like the Firehole, changed my life.

As I've previously mentioned, last summer I was fishing on the North Umpqua, and it was clear there were very few steelhead in the river despite the lateness of the season. Joe Howell, the owner of the Blue Heron Fly Shop, told me that a sprinkling of steelhead had made it into the Camp Water; the few remaining fish were widely scattered in the lower pools downstream to the Famous Pool.

I fished for three days straight without touching a steelhead. I doubt I encountered more than a dozen anglers in all that time. One of those fishermen was Lee Spencer, who had been on the river fishing daily since May. He told me he hadn't had a single hook-up the entire time.

The next morning, while fishing the extreme upper end of the flats above Deadline Falls, a steelhead seized my streamer fly so hard the ten-pound-test leader snapped. It might have been weakened by a wind knot.

The following morning I returned to Deadline and saw another angler planted in the same spot where I'd been the day before. The man was manipulating a two-handed Spey rod. I watched him hook up to a fish twice. Those fights were brief—both times the steelhead came off within seconds. But this was a very encouraging sight. I had the feeling that my fortunes were about to change.

And so I began to fish with an ever-greater avidity. I applied all the streamcraft I knew. I fished with the same kind of enthusiasm I'd brought to this, my favorite river, on the first day I saw it eleven years ago. And yet after all my efforts, all my attention to detail, my renewed enthusiasm, I still failed to take a steelhead on that trip.

None of that matters. What matters is that we are moved by our sport. What matters is that we are touched by all this. Woody Allen once said something to the effect that 90 percent of life is just showing up. Well, fishing is just mostly a matter of being on the water.

Never do I fish as attentively as when I'm on the North Umpqua. I feel I owe the river the very best I have to offer; after all, the river has given its very best to me. The North Umpqua makes me want to be a better fly fisherman.

This is the journey I took to become that better fly fisherman.

One

CONFESSIONS OF A NEW JERSEY TROUT FISHERMAN

Between the conception
And the creation
Between the emotion
And the response
Falls the Shadow

—T. S. Eliot, "The Hollow Men"

New Jersey is no place to live if you're a serious trout fisherman with a bad case of wet brain. The trout fishing is a joke. I know firsthand. I once made my home there.

I made my living as a newspaper reporter. I love nature, but as a journalist I understood that the idyll of trout fishing takes place in a world where dogs still get run over by cars.

I lived on the southern fringe of the New Jersey Pine Barrens. I don't know what your image is of New Jersey, but the rural southern half, with its pine forests and shore towns, is a world apart from the industrialized north. The Pine Barrens account for about one-quarter of the state, a sandy scrubland about the size of Rhode Island. It's a little-known and curious terrain of pitch pines, blackjack oak, Atlantic white cedar, blueberry bushes, and cranberry bogs. Its chief attractions are forest fires and highly contrived stories about the Jersey Devil, a leather-winged demon with a face like a bat or the body of a kangaroo, depending on which version of the story you happen to hear. The Jersey Devil is supposed to fly around the woods at night and has been spotted by everyone from hermits to New Jersey state troopers. The Pine Barrens have always held a sinister attraction for outsiders. The Mafia is said to have dumped more bodies in the Pine Barrens than in New York's East River.

Ask anyone in New Jersey and they'll tell you that the Pine Barrens today are inhabited by an inbred race of dangerous swamp feebs known as Pineys who jacklight deer, make blueberry liquor, and marry their relations. In summer a Piney is recognizable by pale limbs covered in mosquito bites. Pineys have been hiding out in the woods since the American Revolution, when they sided with the British. Modern legend has it that Pineys shot down the *Hindenburg,* believing the airship was manned by revenue agents spying on their stills. Naturally, some of my best friends are Pineys.

Driving south out of the Pine Barrens toward my home in Estell Manor, rural New Jersey takes on the look of the American South. As the pine belt disappears, the southern aspect shows plainly: lowlands and muddy tidal creeks and small patch farms with rows of tomatoes, pumpkins, and corn. There are no trout streams in the Pine Barrens—no trout rivers at all in southern New Jersey. The soil is too sandy, the water too acidic and cedary—conditions that severely limit a trout fisherman.

I had a friend at the newspaper where I worked named Kevin Shelly. Like me, he was a gritty, streetwise reporter who never let his love of nature stand in the way of a good story or a lurid headline. And like me, he also enjoyed fly fishing for trout.

The most important piece of tackle any New Jersey trout fisherman can own is a Pennsylvania fishing license. Fortunately Kevin had close friends, Marco and Donna Aurelio, who resided in the farm country of Cumberland County, Pennsylvania, within easy driving distance of some of the most famous limestone spring creeks in the nation. Their home near Letort Spring Run and the Yellow Breeches became our trout-fishing headquarters.

Marco Aurelio didn't fish. He worked as a Defense Department troubleshooter, an expert in electrical engineering and telecommunications, and he kept on his work desk a volume of the writings of his namesake, Marcus Aurelius. His wife, Donna, worked as a veterinarian's assistant and on the side as a professional fly tier. A whole room in their Mont Alto house had become a fly-tying workshop, and she raised chickens for their capes. I got her started on this kick, having given her my fly-tying vise and materials after discovering I could barely tie the laces on my wading boots, let alone wrap dainty bits of feathers and fur around hooks. Donna was a masterful fly tier and the best fly fisher I'd known. When fishing, she carried a .357 magnum revolver.

A loophole in the Pennsylvania fishing codes allowed anglers to pack heat. This was supposedly for their protection against poisonous snakes. Marco was more worried about snakes of the two-legged variety and insisted that if Donna intended to go out on the streams alone she had better go armed.

If there's a moral in any of this, it's shoot first and ask later what fly they're using. Perhaps this says something about the state of field sports in modern America. At any rate, I came to associate Pennsylvania's spring creeks with gunfire, as we would sometimes take the magnum out for a little target practice before trout fishing. I also came to associate Pennsylvania's spring creeks with mobs of fishermen, another condition of the state of modern fly fishing.

We fished in some of the loveliest rolling farm country imaginable. Our fishing took place behind white limestone barns and farmhouses, stone walls, and manicured pastures set down in fertile valleys between hazy blue mountain ridges. Pheasants cackled in the background. The creeks welled up from fissures in the limestone, rich and weedy and clear as a windowpane.

One spring weekend Kevin, Donna, and I decided to fish the catch-and-release section of the Yellow Breeches behind the famous stone house at Allenberry. That weekend there seemed to be as many people on the river as had been at the original Woodstock. Like me, fully half of them probably carried nonresident fishing licenses. Despite the crowds, I managed to catch a few nice trout.

We fished Falling Spring Run, a clear and fertile limestone stream choked with watercress and dimpling trout. We found

white-winged tricos hatching in the meadow behind the pic-
turesque whitewashed stone house that always seems to crop up
in fishing photographs of this creek, and Donna took several
hefty browns on flies no bigger than the commas on this page.

One day we fished Antietam Creek, a tiny rivulet tumbling
down from the mountains under hanging laurels and rhododendrons; one of the Civil War's bloodiest engagements had been
fought on its banks farther downstream in Maryland. A soft rain
fell, mixing with wet snowflakes. The creek was loaded with small
but truly wild and pretty brook trout, their sides marked with
gemstones swimming in a wash of indigo. Later we drove to a
tavern located just a hundred yards north of the Mason Dixon
line and feasted on fresh blue crabs brought up from the Chesa-
peake Bay. There was a goat tethered to a shed outside, looking
forlorn in the rain.

The most renowned stream in the area, and probably the most
famous trout river in the East after the Catskills' Beaverkill, is
Letort Spring Run, a limestone ditch smelling of honeysuckle
and mud. Fly fishers speak of it as an American Test or Itchen, as
if its brown trout are as smart as Oxford dons. Presumably they've
read Izaak Walton. We found no English dairymaids along its
banks, though there was a concrete interstate highway bridge
spanning the creek, a gravel quarry, the whine of diesel trucks,
and the suburban sprawl of Carlisle. Yet the Letort myth persists.

If trout rivers flowed with irony, the readers of fly-fishing magazines would never get wet.

One weekend in late May, Kevin and I decided to expand our territory and headed for the Poconos in Pennsylvania. Our plan was to fish Big Bushkill Creek, one of the few major Pocono streams still accessible to the public, at the Resica Falls Scout Reservation, six miles of fly-only water managed by the Valley Forge Council of the Boy Scouts of America. For Kevin this was an exercise in nostalgia; as a young Philadelphia-area Boy Scout he had spent many an idyllic summer camping at Resica Falls. We registered at the headquarters below the falls, where the ranger-caretaker hit us up for a "donation" that would be used to help finance stocking.

The Big Bushkill is a typical Appalachian highlands trout river—plenty of pocket water and ledge-rock pools draped with hemlocks and laurels. We were expecting hatches of caddis and maybe some fast-water mayflies, but the regulars facetiously told us that the trout were rising only to the "gypsy moth hatch," a reference to the caterpillar infestation plaguing the Northeast hardwoods that year.

Oak, maple, ash, and a scattering of white pine covered the river's steep banks. Kevin warned me to look out for copperhead snakes as we scrambled over the ledge rocks. The fishing was very slow. I managed to take only one small brown; Kevin, who perversely refused to fish with anything but a dry fly, caught none. We were beginning to regret our lack of gypsy moth patterns.

Returning to the reservation headquarters that evening, we spotted the caretaker-ranger fishing illegally in the forbidden zone at the foot of Resica Falls. There was a deep bend in his fly rod, and we watched as he landed a trout over twenty inches and walked away with it still struggling in his net. Kevin, a hardened newspaperman, was furious, because as a Boy Scout he had helped build a holding pond behind the ranger's house, and he suspected the trout was destined to become the ranger's dinner.

Sooner or later a New Jersey trout fisherman must come to grips with actually fishing within the Garden State itself, though I could never convince Kevin to abandon the celebrated streams of Pennsylvania for the tedious journey north to fish trout streams recognized only for their mediocrity.

Though the drive was torture and the fishing rarely good when I got there, this didn't stop me from wasting untold hours on that scattering of rivers in the rolling mountains and ridge country in the northwestern corner of the state. After all, I had taken my first trout on a New Jersey river.

I don't remember where or when I first got the idea to fly fish for trout. Perhaps like many fly fishers I received my inspiration from a book. I had read the famous trout-fishing scene in *The Sun Also Rises* and Hemingway's short story "Big Two-Hearted River," and those Michigan trout-fishing moments used as mood sweeteners in Robert Travers's *Anatomy of a Murder*. Certainly I fly fished in my head before I ever fished in a trout stream.

I remember once seeing a fly fisherman standing knee-deep in the Musconetcong, the hardwoods leafing out all around him in a riot of springtime. He was casting in a lovely rhythmic motion. I remember it being the most graceful thing I had ever seen. The Musconetcong was the first trout river I ever fished.

There was a no-kill stretch running through Hackettstown where all the fly fishermen gathered. I learned to handle a fly rod by watching these skilled anglers, who seemed to be satisfied with catching lots of small hatchery trout. I asked questions, lots of questions. And so I learned that early in the season, the mayflies hatching on the Musconetcong would be small and dark, and I would need to imitate them fairly closely. As the season progressed, the mayflies grew larger and lighter until June, when the days grew hot and the mayfly hatches all but disappeared, along with the trout. After that the only decent fishing was at dawn and again in the evening. I soon learned that the Musconetcong was filled with tiny cress bugs that resembled a kind of freshwater shrimp. All the nearby sporting goods stores sold these flies, known as "Musky Shrimp."

It was a fraternal crew, crowding each other out of the best holes, free with misinformation and loaned flies that never seemed to match anything actually found in the river. It was the kind of place where a trout tyro such as myself, a New Jersey state trooper, and a longhaired youngster with a cannabis leaf tattooed on his forearm could all fish a pool together, although whether we did this out of friendship or simple overcrowding, I'm not prepared to say. The fishing was absorbing and even beautiful, the trees along the riverbanks in their springtime glory. If you concentrated hard enough you no longer noticed the smell of burning grease coming from the nearby diner or the squeal and rumble of the Hackettstown traffic.

I spent a lot of time exploring the Musconetcong, following twisting country roads, getting lost, and asking for directions from red-eyed tavern owners and gas-station hose jockeys. It was a compromised landscape, with minimalls growing up around old colonial homes that still held grapeshot in the lintels. Many fishermen followed the hatchery trucks, but I had come to think myself too cool for that. On my exploratory drives I noticed that the river had been channeled in many places; the traces of the old canal builders were visible in crumbling locks, collapsed dams, and a straightened streambed.

Then one day another fly fisherman told me about the South Branch of the Raritan River where it flows through the Ken Lockwood Gorge. After a short but confusing drive from Hackettstown to the tiny town of High Bridge, I found the river looking as though it had been lifted from the pages of a pastoral fishing book. It flowed through millraces, past colonial farms and an abandoned iron foundry. A narrow dirt road led up onto the ridge overlooking the river in its beautiful gorge. A private fishing club owned the lower stretch of the river below the gorge; its banks were posted and patrolled, and it looked like something out of a Sparse Grey Hackle story.

The gorge had been named for Ken Lockwood, a New Jersey conservation writer, an oxymoron if ever I heard one. Fishing the pocket waters and riffles, I could fantasize that I was on a truly wild trout stream. An ancient railroad trestle, the remnants of the old Jersey Central Line, disappeared into the woods on the opposite bank. At any moment I half expected to see an iron steam engine come chugging and clattering around a high bend.

Despite visual clues of wildness, the gorge held mostly hatchery trout. Fishermen swore they quickly "naturalized," reverting to wild trout behavior the longer they stayed in the river, but I wasn't buying this for a minute. A hatchery trout is a hatchery trout. If New Jersey trout fishermen excel in any one thing, it is in self-delusion.

Closer to wilderness is the Big Flatbrook, the best trout river in New Jersey. Set in the heart of the Kittatinny Mountains near the Delaware Water Gap, the Flatbrook resembles one of those famous Rip Van Winkle Catskill streams fifty miles to the north.

The Big Flatbrook flows unhindered through the thick forests of the Kittatinnies. Beavers work the banks; white-tailed deer come down to sip at the river before melting back into the woods. You can glimpse a rural yesteryear in nearby villages where blacksmiths, weavers, and potters work at artisan fairs. If you time your vacation wrong, you might run up against an arts and crafts festival put on by these craftsmen, who can't stop weaving baskets and firing bricks. In the 1960s this land had been spared drowning after a huge dam project at Tocks Island on the upper Delaware had been defeated.

My favorite stretch was the Junction Pool, where the Big and Little Flatbrook join. Sometimes I would wander downstream from the village of Wallpack Center to fish the "Rhododendron Stretch," where the water was deep enough to ship into your waders and the banks were walled in by rhododendrons that grew as high as the trees. By mid-May there were good hatches of hendricksons and a sprinkling of the creamy tan mayflies known as March browns. In the evening there were heavy hatches of sulphurs.

But sometime around the middle of June I would become increasingly aware that something was missing in the experience, and over time the thrill of trout fishing began to wear off. I grew tired of long drives to fish overcrowded steams that had to be stocked for there to be any fishing at all. Tired of New Jersey trout streams that were *not* the Catskills. Tired of limestone spring creeks in the Keystone State that did not live up to their hallowed reputations. Tired of rivers where even rangers employed by the Boy Scouts of America poached. Tired of streams where a woman fishing alone had to carry a .357 magnum in order to keep from getting raped.

Between the motion and the act falls the shadow.

One spring day down in the Ken Lockwood Gorge, with the landscape dripping color like an impressionist painting, I asked myself what I was doing there. The beauty that still survived in these few remaining wild places was rapidly shrinking around me. The ravages of so-called progress had left us tone deaf to what remained, blind to rivers draining both nature and history. Maybe it was time to get out. Maybe the Pineys had gotten it right: Go hide in a barrens nobody wants and fish for pickerel and sunfish instead of trout.

Radios blared from cars parked deep in the Ken Lockwood Gorge. Teenagers raced sputtering motorbikes on paths through the woods. Fishermen jockeyed for the best pools.

Human voices wake us, and we drown.

Two

THE WINE OF WYOMING

*T*here is a saying that God created Jackson Hole on the first day, and when he saw how much money he'd spent, he finished the remainder of his creation on a budget.

The Grand Tetons rise without warning seven thousand feet straight up from the valley floor unbuttressed by any foothills, their bold spires nicking the Wyoming sky. The mountains had been named by early French fur trappers, the first white men to gaze upon the peaks. Apparently the fur trappers had gone too long without women. There is a Catholic church in Jackson Hole, once called Our Lady of the Grand Tetons, but eventually rechristened Our Lady of the Mountains after it dawned on someone what the French word *tetons* actually means.

I'd flown into Jackson Hole the night before in the midst of an autumn snowstorm. Late September often brought fresh snow showers into the northern Rockies. As the plane began its descent into the valley of Jackson Hole, suddenly the Tetons were in my face, the craggy peaks poking out of mist and swirling clouds. I had an incredible close-up view of the mountains. And then just as suddenly, as the plane banked, the Tetons rose high above me, and when the plane's wheels touched down on the runway I had to crane my neck to see them.

I was thrilled to be here, on this my first Western trout-fishing vacation. Sooner or later, anyone who is serious about trout fishing in America winds up in this part of the Rocky Mountains, and now it was my turn.

A soft snow blurred Jackson's streetlights and neon motel signs. The town's one traffic light glowed with a soft illumination. Pickup trucks fitted with rifle racks and crackling CB radios passed on streets that were wet but as yet unwhitened. Snow fell silently on the town of Jackson, and I wondered what this might mean for the trout fishing.

"Don't worry, it'll all melt off by noon tomorrow," said my guide, Clark Winston. "Besides, a snowstorm like this gets the trout moving."

Clark had taken me to the Silver Dollar, a saloon tucked away inside the old Wort Hotel, where patrons were shaking fresh snow from their parkas and expensive Sorel boots and the music from the jukebox competed with the din of conversation. Glasses tinkled and bottles glittered along the bar, and the back mirror caught reflections from neon beer commercials. Clark and I shared a table, a pitcher of Coors between us. Clark was going to be guiding me on the Snake River in the morning.

"How come you're not wearing a Stetson, like everybody else in this bar?" I asked him.

"Hell, you know what they say about cowboys—tall in the saddle, short in the jeans."

Like many people who live in Jackson Hole, Clark was not born there. There is a tendency by those "born and bred" to a certain place to feel superior toward newcomers and outsiders. But as Clark was forever telling native Westerners who resented his nouveau presence, he was a citizen of Wyoming by assent, whereas they were merely residents due to an accident of birth. Unlike native Westerners, he said, he had actually gone to some trouble to settle here. The town of Jackson was a melting pot of the New West, tolerant and culturally safe for someone like Clark, who came to Jackson by way of southern California. In many ways Jackson Hole, originally settled by mountain folk and pioneer stock, had come to be a place outsiders had set up for their own comfort and pleasure. Clark was a fishing guide, a member of the Sierra Club, and a contributor to the Jackson Hole Alliance for Responsible Planning. Jackson Hole was famous for its spectacular alpine scenery, ski slopes, and tony affluence, and in this regard was quite different from the rest of Wyoming.

The jukebox was cut suddenly and a quartet of country-rock musicians from Medicine Bow began tuning up on the small bandstand. They looked like sheepherders on heroin. Electric guitars and snare drums caught the light of the beer signs. Glasses and bottles clinked together; the cash register rang. The room was crowded with working ranch hands, local businessmen in fleece-lined jackets, elk hunters, fishing guides, and healthy young folks of both sexes looking very outdoorsy in their jeans and down vests. The band broke into a lament about cheating hearts that seemed to fit the mood of the weather outside in the Rocky Mountain night. The tune was "Jackson Hole Wyoming Is the Coldest Place I Know."

"How's the fishing been?" I asked Clark.

"Do you want the truth or what those liars at the fly shops say?"

"The painful truth."

"Actually, it's pretty good. But hey, the Snake's never going to be in the same league as the Madison or the Henry's Fork."

"Why's that?"

"Our trout just don't grow as big," said Clark. "The Snake River's not as fertile as some of those other streams. The alkalinity's lower and the temperature's colder, too. With all the snowmelt coming off the Tetons, the Snake doesn't even begin fishing well until late summer and fall. But you picked the best time to come out here. You won't believe how beautiful it is on the river right now, with the aspens and cottonwoods changing color."

⌁ ⌁ ⌁ ⌁ ⌁ ⌁

Indeed, the following morning the Tetons appeared fresh and bright under their new dusting of snow. The day was windless and clear. Our first stop was at a local sporting goods emporium so I could buy a nonresident fishing license. The fly shop was located on Jackson's busy town square, with its rustic antler arches and wooden-plank boardwalks. Eighty percent of the jobs in Jackson Hole depended on tourism. The streets were filled with motels, galleries, and souvenir shops, and everywhere I saw signs put up by outfitters advertising float trips on the Snake River. We drove north out of town, Clark's pickup hauling a big McKenzie driftboat on a trailer rig.

"We'll put in at Schwabacher Landing," said Clark. "Float ourselves down to Moose Crossing. Take us the better part of a day. The fishing's not as good as it is in the lower river, but the scenery and wildlife will be worth it."

The Tetons rose off their flat plain, a forty-mile cavalcade of massive, snow-dusted peaks. It was painful to take in the morning light on the snow-edged world. The thin alpine air and brilliant sunshine magnified the gleaming peaks and seemed to bring everything up close, like looking through field binoculars. Each tree in the forests of blue-green lodgepole pine stood out sharply against the snow. I gazed at deeply shadowed ridges segmenting mountains that shone with a steel-blue light. Each passing cloud changed the perspective I had on the glaciers, the hanging valleys, and the fragrant forests. The air was sparkling, the mountain shadows deep, and the spires and their cirques stood out in bold relief.

Our route north followed the sage-covered terraces above the Snake River. Silver-green sagebrush poked out of a dusting of snow that was already melting away under a warming sun. The plain known as Antelope Flats was carpeted by the windblown brush, and I kept alert for the flitting movements of pronghorns.

Brilliant yellow cottonwoods followed the blue artery of the Snake River. The sagebrush plain was interrupted where golden cottonwood trees and reddish bronze willows ran alongside all the streams and watercourses veining the valley. Jackson Hole forms one of the largest enclosed valleys in the Rocky Mountains, roughly sixty miles long, its irregular width varying between six and a dozen miles; from many vantage points along the road I could view the entire expanse. The valley was rimmed by mountains on three sides. Eastward on my right rose the rounded forms of the Gros Ventres, the Washakies, and the Leidy Highlands. The evergreen forests that stood out so boldly at the base of all four mountain ranges were highlighted by patches of flaming aspen groves.

The spruce-scented Snake River flowed over beds of glacial cobblestones, through washes of river gravel, past cooling forests of lodgepole, dividing into many braided channels, a laminar flow whispering under the mountains. Willow flats and beaver-pond marshes spread out from both sides of the Snake. Cottonwoods lined the banks like golden umbrellas that had opened fully.

At Schwabacher Landing, Clark backed the big McKenzie driftboat down to the river's edge and wrestled with the trailer and pulley crank. We would be leaving the truck at the landing and retrieving it at day's end; Clark had arranged for a friend to be waiting for us at Moose Crossing at the end of our float.

We launched ourselves into the smooth but deceptive current. Clark handled the oars with aplomb. The blue river was spangled and sunlit and very tricky, its channels braided and blocked in many places by deadfalls and brush piles. A rookie could get lost or hung up in this maze of channels, but Clark was no greenhorn. "If there's a better way to see the river than by driftboat," he said, "I haven't heard of it." We floated silently past a bank of tall cottonwoods, the mountains coming in and out of view above the trees.

We passed a moose and her calf standing in the willow tangles along the bank, browsing in a dense thicket. An osprey watched us from the skeleton limb of a tree. Clark pointed out mink tracks in the sand and eagles' nests in the cottonwoods.

The river was cold, but the morning air warm. The hairwing dry fly I was floating disappeared in the swirl of a trout's rise. The rod dipped and began pumping against the current. Clark set down the oars and picked up the net. The struggling trout splashed excitedly; I spotted olive and cranberry swirls in the boil. The thrill of that trout transmitting itself to me through the rod was like a first sip of wine.

The trout I brought over to the net had red slashes under its jaw and orangish glow markings on and around the gill plates. Its body was golden olive, with fine black spotting distributed densely toward the tail. A beautiful trout, the Snake River cutthroat.

"Throw that damn trout back—it's mentally retarded," ordered Clark with a laugh. "Some biologist is going to win the Nobel Prize one day after he finds a way to get rid of the stupidity gene in cutthroat trout."

This was a typical prejudice. Cutthroat are the native trout of the Rocky Mountain West, but many fly fishermen regard them as second-class citizens. Cutthroats lack the longevity, size, and fighting strength of brown and rainbow trout. They are also relatively easy to catch and considered unselective and unchallenging by some fly anglers.

"These friggin' cutthroats have given Jackson Hole an inferiority complex," said Clark. "In terms of pure scenery, we have the best trout fishing in the world. But we tend to get defensive about our native cutts. Even Easterners can catch them. Case in point." Clark released my beautiful little cutthroat back into the river.

My rod bent under another struggling cutthroat. This one was larger than the first. A deep orange glow spread out from the gill plates into the belly, and the spots were like a grinding of coarse pepper on the lower flank and tail. These Snake River trout are said to be true aboriginals. Known as the Snake River fine-spotted cutthroat, they are a separate species that can only be found in the drainage fronting the Tetons, from Jackson Lake downriver to the Palisades Reservoir, where the river crosses over the border into Idaho. These Snake River cutts are supposed to be distinguished from their cousins by a profusion of fine spotting on their lower bodies and tails. But there is a question of just how pure these Snake River cutthroat really are. At one time the Snake was stocked with Yellowstone cutthroats, which have larger black spots and are not as brightly colored, and because of this thoughtless act on the part of fisheries managers, many of the trout now found in the Snake may be a kind of cutthroat hybrid. Pure fine-spotted cutthroats unaffected by the Yellowstone strain are said to be found only in some of the remoter creeks, where upstream spawning by river trout was blocked.

"Everyone knows the Snake River isn't what it used to be," said Clark. "I don't care what the other river guides say. The cutthroats just don't grow as big anymore. The river gets too much pressure, especially from guys like us in driftboats. And too many tourists who come out to bother the wildlife, take a leak in the Snake, and then fly back to New Jersey."

Clark said irrigation diversions to ranches also take their toll. It's the Law of the West—ranching takes precedence over wildlife. The levees constructed downstream from the town of Wilson to prevent seasonal flooding channel much of the freedom out of the lower river.

"But the biggest problem is that friggin' dam at Jackson Lake," said Clark.

Jackson Lake is the largest of seven sapphire jewels brimming with snowmelt and trout at the base of the Tetons. A mirror image of the Tetons is reflected in Jackson Lake, which seems to double the height of the mountain range. Gazing into its pristine depths, many people never guess that it's a reservoir and no longer a natural lake. Its first dam was built early in the century, and it was controversial even back then. Because it's the uppermost reservoir in the Snake River system, Jackson Lake is drawn down last, and this is done only rarely. Consequently the beautiful lake escapes the drained bathtub-ring effect that disfigures so many reservoirs. Dark pines surround the shores; the alpine waters are breathtaking.

Near the riverbank a gentle domestic scene was taking place: A moose was coaxing her calf to swim the river. The willows along the banks were every shade of autumn ruddiness. By now the snow had pretty much melted off the river terraces. Clark continued to expound on the horrors of Jackson Dam while I drank in all the beauty.

"With uniform flows coming from the dam year-round," he said, "we've practically eliminated the downstream flooding that moves the river back and forth between the banks and cuts out new channels. A river needs that back-and-forth sawing and shifting to renew riparian vegetation. Moose and other animals depend upon on that vegetation for food. The river gets less braiding and fewer new channels, so we don't have the kind of large sandbars that you see upriver above the lake. Cottonwoods need those sandbars in order to survive. You can see the spruce edging out the cottonwoods down here."

Despite Clark's remarks, I found the river to be a feast for my eyes and brimming with cutthroats. The flies coaxed them up from underneath brush piles and logjams along the banks; or resting where the current eased around submerged stones and boulder stops; holding in the pools that the current had gouged out below islands; and in seams of water that formed between slower and faster currents. The trout I caught were small to medium sized. The glittering stream was a heart-thumping, mind-blowing rush.

Drifting along the riverine corridor, past meadows rimmed with cottonwood trees and aspen groves, I counted beavers, migrating ducks, blue herons, and even a pair of rare trumpeter swans. The Tetons kept bursting into view around the bends. We were under the cluster known as the Cathedral Group. The bent horn of Grand Teton stood out above the other peaks. But for me the most intriguing mountain was Teewinot, which stood slightly in the foreground.

Clark beached the driftboat and we waded into glittering riffles where two channels merged. A grove of aspens on a ridge above us shivered in the wind. Bordered by dark green conifers, the slender white aspen trunks appeared chaste, almost virginal.

The golden leaves were sun-splashed, and there was a lemony light in the grove. The flat leafstalks turned on the slightest breeze, presenting both sides of the leaf to the sunlight. The resultant quivering rustle made a sound a little like a waterfall. John Muir once said that the clearest way into the universe is through a wilderness forest. I would say the clearest way into the universe is through an aspen grove.

I insisted that Clark fish. His silken casting was beautiful to watch. He took three trout to my one. "We're in the temple of the gods," he said.

We ate our lunch sitting on a gravel bar in the sunshine. I saw an incredible scene: A bald eagle skimmed the river and rose with a cutthroat in its talons. The afternoon was intensified by the sky's deep wash of autumn blueness. Although the sun was bright and the light on the water a confection, we could sense waves of cold waiting to descend from the mountain peaks.

"Sometimes a grizzly will wander down here from Yellowstone," said Clark. "A grizz mauled a hunter in these mountains last year."

"If I see a bear, I'll run," I said.

"A grizzly will always outrun a man," said Clark.

"Yes, but I'll bet I can outrun you."

We drifted downriver, exploring braided channels, maneuvering the driftboat back and forth across the riparian corridor. The hairwing drys continued to produce their share of cutthroats. By late afternoon the sun was shining low over the Tetons, casting a glare on the river. We discovered a flat where trout were rising to a hatch of tiny mayflies. It was perhaps the last major hatch of the season, and the first true insect hatch I'd seen all day. We got out of the boat and fished it while it lasted.

We finished our float at twilight, the sun now behind the Tetons. It grew cold quickly; I was shivering by the time we put in at Moose Crossing. A dark oceanic night was gathering over Jackson Hole.

A frosty glittering fall morning dawned on Wyoming. Coming out West to fish for trout was exactly as I had imagined it would be. Life certainly was living up to all its expectations.

My plan that day was to fish Flat Creek in the elk refuge. I had been told that it was there I would find the world's only intelligent cutthroat trout: They actually would be difficult to catch.

Flat Creek is a ribbon of water that winds through a gorgeous and remarkably flat meadow just outside the town of Jackson. The creek drains the National Elk Refuge, the main winter feeding ground of the world's largest elk herd. The great herd of Jackson Hole was still summering in the high country, most of them in Yellowstone Park. When the first heavy snows came, they would begin the migration to Jackson Hole, crossing the snowy valley by the hundreds. As many as fifteen thousand elk would be gathered in Jackson Hole by midwinter. But now they were scattered in the high country, and the rutting season was upon them. From time to time you could hear the distant bugling of bull elk up in the hills.

My first experience of Jackson Hole had been the previous March, to sample the spring skiing. I had seen the great Jackson Hole herd assembled in the winter pasture at Flat Creek, and the sight was as breathtaking as the view of the Tetons. Through midwinter and early spring, elk shed their antlers (quickly growing back another pair). And each spring a local Boy Scout troop picked the National Elk Refuge clean, gathering antlers by the truckload. The scouts sold the elk horn at auction in Jackson's town square. Of late the highest bidders had been representatives of Asian businessmen who were purchasing the horns for their supposed aphrodisiacal qualities. The Boy Scouts were selling elk horn so Asian businessmen could get hard-ons.

Flat Creek passed in looping twists through a treeless meadow that drank the morning sunlight. The stream was indeed as flat and clear as a picture window. That wasn't always the case with the spring creek. In late summer the affluent ranchers around Jackson Hole drew far too much water out of the Gros Ventre River, a tributary of the Snake, which flushed some of the left-over discharge—along with its silt—into Flat Creek. Cattle are king in Wyoming, and the irrigation of ranchland takes precedence over wildlife habitat. The cattlemen have seen to it that this was actually written into the water compacts. "I've never met a Wyoming politician," Clark had told me the other day, "who wasn't related to a cow."

Ranching in Jackson Hole was carried out on a tiny scale in the early years. The cattle business might have been the backbone of Jackson Hole's economy in those days, but nobody was getting rich at it. The family-sized ranches were mostly submarginal, growing barely enough hay to get the livestock through the winter. Ranching in Jackson Hole never operated on a large scale as it did throughout the rest of Wyoming. Even with ranching, there was very little money to be made in Jackson Hole overall.

But as the nineteenth century drew to a close, more and more wealthy Easterners began showing up for the superb elk and big-game hunting, and guiding provided an important source of income to valley residents. Even in its founding days, Jackson Hole was catering to Eastern dudes. With the advent of the twentieth century, a new kind of ranching began taking place in the valley: dude ranching. Many of the outfits that once only ran cattle discovered that Eastern greenhorns were willing to pay good money to board at ranches and play cowboy. Many were so enchanted with the wild and beautiful country, and with the friendly, down-to-earth Westerners who treated them as members of their own family, that they returned each summer. A casual, informal atmosphere prevailed: Dressing up for dinner meant changing your jeans.

One Easterner who settled down here was Strothers Burt, a novelist and pioneer conservationist, who established the Bar BC, one of the earliest and best-known dude ranches in Jackson Hole. His guests included Ernest Hemingway. Burt played a key role in events that eventually led to the preservation of much of Jackson Hole as a national park. John D. Rockefeller Jr. secretly bought up land through a straw purchaser. The land was then donated to the federal government so Franklin Roosevelt could turn much of Jackson Hole into a national monument. Ranchers, enraged by Roosevelt's presidential fiat and armed with rifles and tubs of iced beer, led a wild cattle drive of 650 yearling Herefords across the newly created monument to protest the federal seizure of the open range. They were spurred on by a theatrical and possibly drunken Wallace Beery, who kept a summer home in Jackson Hole. Beery had made a Western in the valley, and the actor liked the views so much he stayed. He appeared astride his horse, wearing the cowboy getup he had worn in his Hollywood shoot-'em-up, a Winchester rifle strapped to the saddle. "Shoot to kill," he allegedly advised the cattlemen who had gathered at the Elks Club in downtown Jackson. But when the mob crossed the monument boundary, there was nobody to shoot at, not a federal official in sight. The cattlemen, who expected to be met by armed federal troops, didn't understand that the government was guaranteeing the ranchers all rights-of-way and full grazing privileges within the national monument. This grazing tradition carried over when the monument was later expanded into Grand Teton National Park, and it exists to this day.

Over time, ranching in Jackson Hole grew more refined to suit tourism. Lumpy bunk beds and drafty cabins gave way to Rancho Deluxe, with chuckwagon lunches, ranch-style barbecues, and square dancing. Horseback riding supervised by wranglers might range from a trip around the paddock to a backpacking expedition into the wilderness. Lately many of the Spin-and-Marty dude ranches have found an additional source of income: opening up their spring creeks to fly fishermen.

Jackson Hole's early settlers had been quick to recognize the value of springs with consistent year-round flows, and they staked their homestead claims around these creeks. Today those who hold the deeds continue to jealously guard their waters. These creeks rise full blown from fertile springheads and are fundamentally different from the freestone rivers in that the temperatures of the water remain fairly constant year-round. Spring creeks stay cool in summer and don't freeze over in wintertime. This makes for a longer feeding season for the trout, which grow to tremendous size during their short life spans. The rich alkalinity of the streams produces heavy weed growth that supports a large insect population—which, in turn, the trout feast upon.

Because there is so much insect life in spring-fed streams like Flat Creek, and because the currents move so slowly, the cutthroat trout are selective in their feeding. That's why fly anglers say that spring creek cutthroat are "smarter" than the average cutthroat and harder to catch. By this they only mean that the trout have time to pick and choose as insects slide by on a slowly moving and remarkably clear dinner tray.

Few streams around Jackson Hole are said to frustrate the angler more often than Flat Creek. The lower portion of the stream flowing through the elk pasture is designated fly fishing only, one of the few such bodies of water in Wyoming to have such a restriction. In order to protect the cutthroat trout that spawn in springtime, Flat Creek is open to anglers only in late summer and autumn. It's a creek that demands a hunting and stalking strategy to visible trout instead of blind, random casting.

I fished where only two lonely cottonwoods grew beside the creek on a flat plain; there was precious little brush. I tried to keep back from the fringe of the stream so as not to panic the trout by my presence. These fish were incredibly spooky. I edged a little closer to the bank for a better look.

Flat Creek's severely bent channel had carved out an extensive series of deep indentations under the sod banks. I could see that some of these undercuts extended as much as three or four feet beneath the banks. Not only did these cutbanks provide cover for the cutthroats, but any vibration on the bank would warn trout of approaching predators.

Dark mayfly duns hatched on the surface. Trout rings appeared and disappeared on the water. The rises occurred tight alongside the banks. I judged the feeding lanes for these rising trout to be less than ten inches wide. Subtle crosscurrents appeared in the stream due to braided weeds, and a westerly breeze kept my fly from landing in the proper current. Extreme delicacy and a cautious approach were necessary. Keeping a low profile, if not exactly kneeling, and keeping as far away from the bank as possible, I tried to time my casts to match the rhythms of individual rises. The trick was to get the fly to pass over the trout at the moment it was ready to open its mouth to a real insect. I played a game of winks and nods with the trout until the dun hatch evaporated. The trout won.

I fished until noon, wanly casting at a creek that had turned off its magical rises. No more hatches. I tied on a cinnamon ant imitation and floated it close to the bank for a while. Then I switched to a small black beetle. At last a sipping cutthroat pulled the fly under. The two-pound trout fought gamely but didn't clear the water, because cutthroat trout don't jump. This is said to be another of their limitations. But I wasn't buying it. For a New Jersey trout fisherman, this was the finest trout fishing on earth.

I took the road out to Moose Junction and Jenny Lake later that afternoon. Jenny Lake is one of those sapphire gems at the foot of the Tetons. The lake is a natural mirror for the mountains. This was the nearest I had come yet to the base of the Tetons. I craned my neck to see peaks rising above the lodgepole forest. Jenny Lake is directly under the cluster known as the Cathedral Group, a concentration of the tallest spires in the mountain chain. Mount

Owen, Mount Teewinot, and Middle and South Tetons gather around the magnificent bent horn of Grand Teton.

I stopped at the Jenny Lake Ranger Station to pick up a special fishing permit for Cottonwood Creek, and the ranger, whose name was Roxanne, assured me that the cutthroats were biting.

The creek ran through a golden corridor of cottonwoods and aspens. A bull elk and his doe were watering a hundred yards downstream. The magnificently antlered bull and the shy doe swung their heads up in unison to stare at me. Their gaze seemed fixed but placid enough. Elk usually keep a distance that varies with their mood. I knew enough not to bother these animals. Bulls are particularly touchy in autumn during the rut. The rack on this bull's head looked like it might weigh upward of fifteen pounds.

A cloud of whirling mayflies swarmed above the creek's riffling shallows. After mating, the insects would drop and die on the stream, and the trout would rise to eat them. Until that time I would fish the stony creek with a Gold-Ribbed Hare's Ear.

I felt a tug on the line and pulled up on a cutthroat. The fish splashed wildly in the stream. There was a pleasing, satisfactory weight on the end of the line. I thought not for the hundredth time how lucky I was to be out here.

A bugle call rang out in the forest. Bull elk frequently square off in fall, pushing each other around with their great racks. In late spring and summer, as new antlers grow out, the racks are covered in tender velvet. The delicate membrane is highly sensitive and bruises easily. The bulls move through the forest with regal grace, taking great care with their antlers, their heads carried erect so that the spreading tines, which grow out of the backs of their skulls, won't catch on branches. But in autumn the males use their hardened racks in sparring matches to determine the right to mate with the females. The sound of their antlers cracking and scraping together is one of the great thrills of a high-country autumn.

I fished into the chill twilight, and the bugling of the elk raised gooseflesh on my arms.

I awakened to a brand new world each morning. The autumn weather was crystalline. There was no need for an early, penitential start on the rivers. This late in the season the best fishing occurs between ten o'clock in the morning and four in the afternoon, when the golden autumn sunshine warms the big Snake River and the trout become most active.

The wide gravel floodplain of the Snake appeared almost white, and the yellow cottonwoods on the shelving bars were in their glory. I fished the braided channels below Hoback Junction, where the Tetons are no longer visible. The river was deep here, but I found good dry-fly fishing along the banks and shelving bars, and I took a beautiful sixteen-inch cutthroat. I stopped at several turnouts to fish the river where the road paralleled the river from Astoria Hot Springs down to West Table Creek. There was plenty of access on U.S. Forest Service land.

This was prime bald eagle habitat, even better than in Grand Teton National Park.

Downriver lay Alpine Canyon. Cliffs dropped to the river; conifers blanketed the slopes. The whitewater rapids began with a whisper. The rapids were foam on green. This is some of the most dramatic whitewater in the Rocky Mountains. Some people call this stretch the Grand Canyon of the Snake River, although it's not nearly as deep as Hell's Canyon of the Snake hundreds of miles downstream on the far side of Idaho.

I fished the green waters of the Hoback River in its conifer canyon and caught some nice cutthroats in the rock and gravel pools. Another morning I drove out to the Gros Ventre River above Slide Lake. I could see the massive scarring on the side of the mountains left by the huge landslide that had dammed the river and created the lake back in the 1920s. I fished the Gros Ventre below Crystal Creek Campground and then wound up on Crystal Creek itself. The cliffs above the creek's banks were covered in tangled brush and wild rose. I didn't catch any trout in Crystal Creek but I enjoyed the sight of water ouzels, or dippers, submerging themselves in the stream. The birds sang chorales to the accompaniment of the rushing creek and immersed their plump gray bodies completely under water in order to walk along the streambed in search of food.

One morning I hiked up into Cascade Canyon to see Hidden Falls. I reached it by an inexpensive boat ride across Jenny Lake.

Cascade Creek poured through a hanging valley, a glacier-cut vale marked by a steep drop at its lower end. The trail climbed for half a mile to a wonderfully tall bridal-veil falls. A plume of mist drifted skyward in a tall curve between the steeply forested cliffs along the waterfall. A short distance on, the trail emerged from the pines at Inspiration Point, giving me a view across Jenny Lake to the Gros Ventre Range on the other side of the valley.

The glaciers—Teton, Skillet, Falling Ice, Triple, and Middle Teton among the largest—still grind and scour the mountains. The lakes below are glacier melt. Like the other lakes in the mountain chain, Jenny was the remnant of a glacier that had inched its way down the canyon.

As the sun set behind the range, I watched the lengthening shadows of the Grand Tetons project themselves onto the floor of Jackson Hole. They spread over the sagebrush flats and up the ridges beyond.

There was an urgency to the season. Ducks and geese flew southward over the river valley in wedges and chevrons. Moose fed with renewed purpose in the willow thickets, and elk grazed intently in the meadows. There was no mistaking the feeling now: The valley was preparing for the white sleep of winter.

Driving back, I spotted pronghorn antelope bounding across the sagebrush. A mule deer flitted across my path. Lights burned warm and yellow in the ranch houses and log cabins. No matter how cold the night became, the sight of those yellow cabin lights always restored me to a sense of comfort. The sky was a diamond field, the haze from the Milky Way a vestigial glow of silver on the peaks of the Tetons.

Early the next morning I went up to fish the Oxbow on the Snake River in Grand Teton National Park. Here were the best views of the Tetons, the views Ansel Adams had photographed. The afternoon was bright, but there was little warmth to the sun; I could feel winter in the wind. Yellow cottonwood leaves blew and fell into the river. On the high ridges, cold winds were stripping the aspens bare. Everything about the day suggested the season was changing fast. I caught no fish at the Oxbow on that day.

The next day a low front descended over seven Western states. The sun couldn't quite penetrate the leaden sky. It looked as if it would either sleet or begin to snow. I was getting grim reports of the fishing on the Snake and on the nearby spring creeks.

Clearly it was time to drive up to Yellowstone Park and fish the Firehole River.

Three

HORN OF PLENTY

I departed Jackson Hole early in the morning under an overcast sky that made the Tetons look dull and slate colored. The headwaters of the Snake form on the Yellowstone Plateau, in the pine-covered moraines around Two Ocean Pass. North of Jackson Lake the sagebrush flats give way to lodgepole forests guarding the entrance to the park. Three times the park road crosses the winding Continental Divide. I trailed behind slow-moving motor homes driven by senior citizens. They were the last of the season's vacationers. Finally this highway took me past Old Faithful and into Upper Geyser Basin on the Firehole River.

Plumes of steam rose above Biscuit Basin, drifting into the screen of lodgepoles fringing the meadow. Both Iron Spring Creek and the Little Firehole poured into the main river, contributing to the chill currents. Below Biscuit Basin serpentine bends cut channels in the meadows before disappearing behind a thick stand of pines.

The Firehole in Biscuit Basin was as smooth and clear as windowpane, with weeds twining under water against a bottom of black volcanic sand. Its beds were so choked in some places with fountain moss and emerald chara weed that what at first appeared on the surface to be a smooth current was on closer inspection a complication of many swirls and confusing currents.

After a week of fishing for cutthroats in Jackson Hole, I was more than ready for the greater sport of brown trout fishing. In fact, you could say I was in a brown trout state of excitment. The rivers of Yellowstone had been planted in the nineteenth century with European brown trout and coastal California rainbows. These foreign trout had supplanted the native cutthroats in many of the park's rivers. At one time the Firehole had been barren of trout; fish couldn't migrate above its waterfalls. Now it's one of the best trout rivers on earth—and, because of its geyser fields, one of the most surreal and beautiful.

Trout thrive in the incredibly clean and transparent springwaters. At Biscuit Basin, in a bend between a pair of steam-bleached deadfalls, trout rose to insects so small that at first I couldn't see them. They were *Baetis*.

I didn't have anything in my fly box small enough to match them. My leader, caught up in the opposing currents created by the waterweeds, dragged my fly across and finally under the surface. This motion didn't seem to scare the trout; they must have been aware of my presence, however, because they consistently ignored all my ham-handed offerings.

I followed the Firehole as it unspooled like a ribbon through the lodgepoles. Where thick stands of pine and spruce provided more gloom on an already dark day, I managed to take a few small trout in the riffles and broken-bottom pools. The river here cut through a narrow valley between two heavily forested plateaus. The riverbed was composed of a curious thin crust of black lava known as rhyolite. These lava ledges and crusts were worn smooth in some places, pockmarked in others. Steam rose out of vents in banks formed by a whitish mineral accretion known as sinter, a crust of silica and other mineral deposits created by runoff from discharging geysers and hot springs. Algae and brightly colored lichen bloomed on rocks where the steaming seepages trickled into the river. In the water below Upper Iron Bridge, the Firehole passed along a pine-bordered meadow in a long riffle and run before reaching the head of a gleaming quarter-mile oxbow known as Muleshoe Bend.

From the parking turnoff on the high bluff overlooking Muleshoe Bend, I spotted exactly what I had been hoping to see. The bend's smooth surface was broken by dozens of dimples and circles, forming and disappearing on the moving water. I scrambled down the slope to find trout rising freely to more tiny *Baetis*. My luck held better than at Biscuit Basin. I seemed to be getting the hang of things now. It took a stealthy approach, a slack line, and a thin and supple leader to deceive the brown and rainbow trout in these weedy currents.

A pot of boiling springwater bubbled up from the bank at the lower end of Muleshoe Bend. The river swept around ledge-rock shallows toward the billowing steam clouds of Midway Geyser Basin. I managed to catch small rainbow trout in the riffles directly above the stretch of river where Excelsior Geyser discharged thousands of scalding gallons into the Firehole by the minute. The banks were obscured in plumes of steam.

Below the Midway footbridge the river looped back into the forest and away from the highway. The valley and lodgepole bench at Goose Lake Meadows was, to my mind, the most beautiful stretch on the Firehole. Here the river was a long smooth glide with deeply undercut banks and marshy bottoms. Unexpected potholes and cold springs refreshed the stream.

Downstream the river glided over shallow lava stair-steps, slowing into a deep hourglass pool before looping around the meadow at Elk Springs. It then meandered in long sweeping bends through the grassy meadow flats until coming to a series of tumbling chutes and faster water that climaxed in a small falls and plunge pool. This pocket water was said to have an indifferent reputation among anglers, but I managed to catch modest-sized rainbows and brown trout in its rocky fissures.

Below this run the Firehole rounded a tight bend near the old Fountain Freight Road just above the iron footbridge at the steaming geyser known as Ojo Caliente, the hot eye. From this geyser spring warming the river, with its billowing steam clouds, downstream two hundred yards to a boggy island at the mouth of Fairy Creek, the channel was filled with thick weed beds that held numerous trout rising to tiny sedges and mayflies. A little farther downstream Sentinel Creek spilled into the river, and trout held tight to the bank below its cold mouth. Sentinel drained a small subalpine meadow and pine forest below a pitch-stone escarpment, and I took some time to explore behind its screen of lodgepoles in search of brook trout.

At Lodgepole Bend the Firehole looped back toward Fountain Freight Road. At Fountain Flats trout rose in weedy channels to sip mayfly hatches. Steam seeped out of vents in the meadows. Hot vapor escaped from the crusted banks along the stream. I shared the meadow with one of Yellowstone's bison herds. The beasts stood dumbly, silently under the falling snow, their breath steaming in the cold air. A deep funnel-shaped pool waited for me below Fountain Flats; it was here that I broke off a large trout because I failed to remove a wind knot from my leader.

Nez Perce Creek entered the Firehole below Fountain Flats. Below the creek, in its last three miles, the Firehole changed dramatically in appearance, giving up most of its thermal features.

Sheltered by a dense lodgepole forest and known in this stretch as the Broads, the river appeared imminently fishable, passing in smooth, fairly uniform glides over a rich weedy bottom.

There was little warning of the Firehole Cascades. The river narrowed between high lodgepole cliffs, suddenly dropping into foaming staircases. Whitewater rapids stood out against a dramatic backdrop of dark canyon walls and thickly clustered lodgepoles. Below the Cascades, Firehole Falls dropped into a stunning rock-strewn glen, thundering and foaming beneath black lava cliffs and dark evergreens. Beneath this uproar the river calmed, slowing as it wound through a beautiful bunchgrass meadow where the Firehole and Gibbon rivers joined to form the Madison.

I fished the Firehole for a week in something very close to a fugue state. The sun was a pale wafer behind gray clouds and rising steam. The hot spillage from the geysers constantly poured into the river and kept the Firehole from becoming too cold in the chill October air. Often I would stop fishing long enough to wade over to a bank and warm my wet, numb hands over a hot pool or in the steam escaping from a fumarole. And I looked forward at night to the comfort of a motel room in the town of West Yellowstone.

One bitter afternoon the Firehole seemed lifeless. The river was the color of lead. It was a good bet that the trout fishing was pretty much over for the season. I decided to try Fountain Flats; it was always the last holdout for rising trout when the rest of the river seemed lifeless. Steam drifted in clouds above the flats. Rags of mist drifted through the pines. Dark clouds threatened snow squalls.

For a time the wind stopped blowing. It grew eerily still. I was surprised to see the dimples and circles of rising fish down to a bend where the river disappeared behind the lodgepoles. I waded into the water. It seemed strange that I felt warmer standing waist-deep in this river than I did standing on the bank. I fished for the rising trout with mixed results.

The hatch didn't last. Suddenly I was engulfed in snow. The steam billowing on the wind looked surreal in the pale light of the squall. I climbed shivering out of the river. Steam from the fumaroles drifted into the pines. I took off my waders, pulled on a heavy parka, and climbed behind the front seat of my car.

The basin beyond the trees had filled with many bison. The winter herd was gathering. They stood silently in the falling snow. Steam rose off their flanks, and their breath steamed, too. The effect was like looking at one of the geyser fields. The snowy river bottom had filled up entirely with dark bison. The scene was so still and calm that I stayed to look at the animals for a long time. The herd was so silent that I felt I had been lifted into another world.

I took a room in the Alpine Motel in West Yellowstone. It was a gateway town, ideally situated at the West Entrance to Yellowstone Park. It was also dead center within a hundred-mile radius of what I was quickly discovering to be the finest trout fishing in America.

I hung out at Bob Jacklin's and Bud Lilly's fly shops. I felt a special affinity for Jacklin's shop, because Jacklin came from New Jersey. I ate chicken-fried steaks at Huck's Diner and at the Totem Cafe. I drank Coors beer at the bar in the Stagecoach Inn. You couldn't buy Coors back East at that time; it had a wholly undeserved cult following. All of West Yellowstone's shops and cafés had photographs hanging up on their walls showing winter snowdrifts piled up to the roof. Just in case you had any ideas about moving out here. Basically I used West Yellowstone to eat, sleep, and buy trout flies. But mostly I fished from first light to first dark.

From my headquarters at West Yellowstone, I was able to explore trout waters both in and around the park. The road north led to the Gallatin and Madison rivers in Montana. I could drive south through the park to fish the Snake River in front of the Grand Tetons. Or drive north along the Yellowstone River where it left the park, crossed Wyoming into Montana, and flowed into Paradise Valley under the Absaroka Mountains. And a quick drive east over Targhee Pass into Idaho would bring me to the placid meadow waters of the Henry's Fork of the Snake River on the famous Railroad Ranch. The Henry's Fork soon became my favorite destination.

The lodgepole forests opened up onto the expansive sagebrush flat that was Harriman State Park, the old Railroad Ranch. In the morning I would park near the fence boundary and begin the long walk across the luxuriant meadow. Halfway across the flat I'd pause for a look behind me. In the distance I could see the outline of Last Chance, with its pair of fly shops, single motel, and gas station. Last Chance got its name because in the old days it was the last chance to buy gas between here and Jackson Hole. Behind the buildings of Last Chance were the dark pines of the Yellowstone Plateau. And from where I stood I could see over into Wyoming where the pale, jagged outline of the Tetons was clearly visible. Here was the western perspective of those mountains as seen from Idaho, in some ways the more interesting view. The peaks seemed to float weightless far in the distance, a pale blue color like smoke.

Waterfowl summered over in the ranch's irrigation ditches. Long-billed curlews made clacking noises in the high grass. Sandhill cranes burst out of hiding and startled me with screams that carried for half a mile. I saw a bald eagle circling the distant ranch buildings.

After a fifteen-minute walk, I came upon the bank of the giant meadow stream. It was a broad expanse of water, ninety yards wide and entirely wadable, flowing by with barely a whisper. The morning sunlight over the placid river had filled with swarms of tiny, fluttering, white-winged insects. All across the smooth, broad surface I could see insect life awash on the current. Tiny mayflies, delicate, soft-bodied insects with gauzy wings held upright, floated on the braided currents. The trout bulged and dimpled and made soft slurping sounds.

I sniffed the sage-scented breeze and looked out over an un-spoiled landscape. The Henry's Fork is quite possibly the loveliest piece of trout real estate on earth. It is said that no trout river sees as many different mayfly emergences as the Henry's Fork. For a dry-fly fisherman it is the horn of plenty.

Thick waterweeds wave gently in the ambling currents. Pods of free-rising rainbow trout work up and down the slicks, feeding on complex insect hatches. It seems that insects are continuously hatching and trout always rising on the Henry's Fork. In their adult stage the insects live for only a few hours or days. At their aquatic larval stage they can last for several years. The trout feed on both stages in the existence of these mayflies. I've never had much interest in stream eutomology or hatch-matching, but what I saw on the Henry's Fork took my breath away.

The first major mayfly hatch of the spring is *Baetis tricaudatus,* tiny insects known to fly fishermen as iron blue quills. The duns start hatching in late March on the Henry's Fork and continue coming off the river sporadically until the end of May. These duns hatch in their greatest numbers in late morning on overcast days. The blue quills offer superb early-season fishing in spring. The *Baetis* hatch resumes in autumn and can produce outstanding dry-fly fishing in cold weather.

The large mayflies known as Rhithrogena, or black quills, be-gin hatching in April and provide some fast action when the general fishing season opens in May down in the Last Chance area. They're best imitated with the artificial flies known as Mahogany Duns and Dark Quill Gordons.

The most important mayfly hatch in the West begins in early June on the Henry's Fork, when the pale morning duns (*Ephemerella inermis*) struggle to the surface on the ranch water. The yellow-green mayflies get smaller as the season wears on. In June mating swarms fall in the morning, just before duns start hatching on the water. By August the duns can be seen coming off at midday, and the trout feed selectively on emergers just below the surface.

Sometime around the third or fourth week of June the most famous mayfly emergence on the Henry's Fork gets under way. This is the western green drake hatch (*Drunella grandis*), drawing fly anglers from all over the nation and abroad, and it lasts about two weeks. These large mayflies seem to bring up every big trout in the river. The rainbows feed greedily as the drakes emerge. On warm sunny days the duns hatch in late morning. On cold overcast days they hatch at midafternoon. The mating swarms occur in the morning hours, and these large spinners bring up just as many trout as the duns. The greatest crowds tend to descend on Railroad Ranch during the green drake hatch, and although that might be unpleasant, the fishing can be breathtaking.

To avoid the mob on Railroad Ranch during the green drake hatch, you can always drive downriver below the town of Ashton and fish their cousins, the gray drakes (*Siphlonurus occidentalis*). The best fishing with these large insects occurs in the evening during spinner falls if you can match the hatch successfully with an old-fashioned dry fly like a size 10 Adams.

The largest mayflies that hatch on the Henry's Fork are the brown drakes (*Ephemera simulans*). The duns hatch and the spinners fall at dusk. It's a challenge to figure out what stage of the mayfly the trout are feeding on. Brown drakes favor silty riverbeds, so the best hatches on the Henry's Fork occur at the southern end of Railroad Ranch, where the current is at its slowest.

At the tail end of the green drake hatch a similar but smaller green drake comes off the Henry's Fork water, the small western green drake (*Ephemerella flavilina*). Peak hatch activity usually occurs in mid-July. Duns hatch in the afternoon; spinners fall in the morning and evening. Western Olive No Hackles and Rusty Spinners are suitable imitations for both duns and spent insects.

Sometimes during late-June and July afternoons, when larger and more prominent mayflies are hatching on the Henry's Fork, a smaller *Baetis* mayfly known as the tiny blue quill will appear, although it's often overlooked by fly fishermen. That's too bad, because there can be good fishing to this hatch with very small Rusty Spinners.

Sometimes during summer rain showers tiny blue-winged olives (*Pseudocloeon edmundsi*) will appear on the water in great numbers. This blue-winged olive hatch intensifies by late summer, until they carpet the water in the chill of September. The trout can become very picky while sipping these tiny insects.

In August a mayfly usually associated with lakes, the speckled spinner (*Callibaetis ferrugineus*), shows up in the slower, weedier sections of Railroad Ranch. The spinners descend in heavy concentrations during late-morning hours. An old-fashioned Adams fly often gets the job done.

By September on the flat sections of the Harriman Ranch water, *Tricorythodes* s—extremely tiny, white-winged flies with black thoraxes—often produce the very best fishing of the morning. The trico duns start hatching in the early-morning hours; spinner falls hit the water soon after.

Another important hatch is the mahogany dun (*Paraleptophlebia*). Fly fishermen consider the mahogany dun the preeminent hatch of September—and it takes only a few insects to get the trout feeding. Trout sip them eagerly, regardless of their numbers. The duns hatch in midmorning. But even by afternoon, when the duns are long gone and smaller blue-winged olives cover the water, selective trout still might choose an angler's mahogany dun imitation.

Those are the significant mayfly hatches. The Henry's Fork teems with other aquatic insects, too. There seem to be as many species of caddisflies as mayflies. In April swarms of caddis appear in the afternoon and evening hours on the Henry's Fork well downriver from the ranch below the town of Ashton. Unlike the

Railroad Ranch water, this section is open to fishing year-round, and the caddis produce excellent action for fly fishermen.

When the general fishing season opens on the Memorial Day weekend you can find excellent hatches of large caddis on the area of the river at Last Chance directly above the Harriman Ranch water.

When Railroad Ranch opens to fishing on June 15, caddis activity can be quite intense. The best hatches occur in the late-afternoon and evening hours, but caddis also hatch in the morning at the same time that pale morning duns are coming off the river.

In July spectacular caddis flights occur nearly every evening on the Henry's Fork on Railroad Ranch. Several species of caddis can be seen both hatching and laying eggs at the same time. A small Partridge Caddis works well to imitate the many spent caddis drifting downriver.

By the first of August the principal caddis hatches are over. But by mid-August a very important late-evening caddis hatch comes off, producing some of the best fishing of the year.

In September a final caddis hatch remains, though its presence is a secret known only to a few fishermen. Anglers have to get up pretty early in the morning to see it. In the slow sections of the river a dark-colored caddis hatches only in the predawn gray. It's usually over by the time most anglers make it down to the river.

In addition to mayflies and caddis at Railroad Ranch, stoneflies hatch upriver in the fast water of Box Canyon during May and June. A hatch of large stoneflies known locally as the salmonfly hatch draws anglers from all over to the canyon. A smaller insect called the golden stonefly hatches right after the big salmonflies. In Box Canyon this golden stone hatch continues into August.

Aquatic flies are not the only insects of interest. Terrestrials such as grasshoppers, ants, and beetles are very important to fly fishermen on the Henry's Fork, especially on the ranch water. On days when gusting winds keep down the insect hatches and drive most fishermen from Railroad Ranch, a hopper imitation dropped tight against a bank will often save the day. And there have been September days when I found that large bank feeders seemed to prefer red or black ants and beetles over mayflies.

In those days when I first fished Railroad Ranch, the larger trout ran to twenty inches or more. I found them tough to hook, tough to play, tough to land. The rules called for fly fishing only, with barbless hooks. Catch-and-release was the code of the river, if not yet the law.

The rainbow trout have a lot of time to pick and choose what they want to eat in those slow currents. Several different insect species might be hatching or laying eggs at any one time. Fly fishermen have observed as many as a *dozen* different hatches going on all at once on this river. Many times during these complicated masking hatches I couldn't tell exactly what the fish were feeding on, and it was all I could do to catch trout. I had to observe with great care to see which insects the trout preferred. The Henry's Fork trout establish feeding patterns and can be single-minded in their foraging, choosing one species of insect over another.

I once experienced a rainy day on the Henry's Fork when so many tiny blue-winged olives carpeted the water that I could no longer see my own fly among them. On other days trout fed on barely visible tricos while ignoring larger mayflies. It was a case of too many choices for both trout and fishermen on the Henry's Fork. May all your problems be like these.

In the Railroad Ranch the Henry's Fork's fertility, its nearly infinite mayfly hatches, its steady flow, and its wadable bottom have made this giant meadow stream the finest stretch of trout water anywhere. Surely this is the best dry-fly fishing on earth.

I have never seen a lovelier ranch meadow. On clear days you can see for miles across the high basin of the lodgepole country. The pale outline of the Tetons appears far away above lesser foothills darkened by timber.

The Railroad Ranch was once the property of Edward Henry Harriman and his Union Pacific Railroad. Harriman was granted the deed to the acreage in exchange for laying the railroad track into West Yellowstone. The Harriman family always granted the public the right to fish on Railroad Ranch. After the death of Roland Harriman the ranch was presented outright to the citizens of Idaho as a gift. It was possibly the nicest thing rich people have ever done for their fellow Americans.

I would pack a lunch down to the river and spend an entire day fishing the five miles of ranch water. Trout would be rising and dimpling all around me. Choosing the right fly was a delightful problem to be solved. In time I discovered through close observation that the larger rainbow trout were not among the fish rising to insects at midstream. I began to look for tiny bubble trails along the embankments. A really large trout searching for nymphs on the bottom would release an almost invisible chain of bubbles. It was a dead giveaway to the trout's presence, if you knew what to look for. One afternoon a lunker rainbow lying close by the bank and releasing bubbles seized my cinnamon-colored ant. My Pflueger's clicking mechanism screamed before the leader snapped.

I met a lot of really interesting fishermen on the Henry's Fork. A mustached adolescent from Sun Valley showed me his daddy's bamboo fly rod. He had inherited it from the old man; it had taken lots of trout in its day. "The fishing up in Sun Valley is just as good as it is here and in Yellowstone Park," the boy assured me, with regional pride in his voice. I made a mental note to get up to Silver Creek.

I met Cecil, my first trout bum. Cecil lived in Chicago and drove a hack when he worked, which was seldom. He spent each summer and fall season in its entirety fly fishing the Yellowstone country. He didn't have a pot to piss in, but he owned a vintage bamboo fly rod. He had been variously sleeping in his pickup truck, sleeping in a rented tepee, and sponging off a girlfriend in Caspar, Wyoming. He drank Gallo Chablis from a chipped coffee mug, and on the evening I met him insisted on trying to teach me how to imitate the trumpeting cries of a bull elk in rut. "I feel mournful whenever I hear that sound," said Cecil, cupping his hands and emitting a series of loud high squeals. "Now isn't that just the most beautiful sound in the world?"

Cecil was a true crank and he cared for little except fly fishing. He showed me how the game was played on the Henry's Fork, making downstream presentations of a dry fly to rising trout on the slow-moving ranch water; previously I had been casting exclusively upstream to rising fish, the way they teach you in books. "You get a longer drift," Cecil explained.

Cecil took the trouble to give me an itinerary of rivers to fish in the Yellowstone country.

—"The Firehole might just be the most beautiful trout stream in the West."

—"Look for brown trout in the meadows of the Gibbon River. You'll see lots of elk there. They come down to the river to drink in the evening."

—"Hike in to Slough Creek. Some of the best scenery in the world is up there in those meadows."

—"In autumn brown trout swim out of Hebgen Lake to spawn in the Madison River. Fish Beaver Meadows and the holes behind the Barns."

—"There are more cutthroats on the Yellowstone River around the Buffalo Ford area in Yellowstone Park than anyplace else in the world."

—"The Madison River outside the park is a fifty-mile trout riffle from Quake Lake down to Ennis."

—"Float the Beaverhead to catch the biggest brown trout in Montana."

—"Fish the Big Hole in its haystack valley. The best fishing is in June for the salmonfly hatch, and again in September for brown trout below the town of Melrose."

—"The Bitterroot is one of Montana's most beautiful streams. Fish it on the way to Missoula."

—"Rock Creek is a classic. See the canyon when the aspens are changing color in the fall."

—"Spend a few days around Livingston in Paradise Valley. Fish the Yellowstone at Mallard's Rest. The river looks wonderful under the Absarokas."

—"The Henry's Fork on the Harriman Ranch is the most beautiful meadow river in the West. You have to envy the Harrimans."

But I already knew how beautiful the Henry's Fork could be. I couldn't keep my eyes off the gorgeous meadow ranch or the distant views of the Tetons. Photographs had not, could not, do justice to the Henry's Fork. Sometimes when the trout were rising in the Millionaire's Pool, or in the Back Channels, or on a stretch known as Bonefish Flats, I would drop into a state of concentration known only to fly fishermen in which I was oblivious to anything beyond casting range. And then I would look up and see the meadow drinking up the sunlight, and hear geese overhead calling down. Or I might spot white pelicans on the water, or see a weasel shading its eyes over on the bank. Or maybe the evening star would be coming out as I waded from the river, shivering.

I couldn't get enough of Railroad Ranch. But I caught my largest Henry's Fork trout in Box Canyon. The Box is a tough place to get into, with steep brushy banks, an unforgiving current, and a cobble-and-rock bottom that's tough to wade safely.

On a bitterly chill autumn morning, as a miserable drizzle fell out of a gray sky, I climbed down into Box Canyon to fish. I tied on a large black stonefly imitation called a Bitch Creek Nymph. That was the popular stonefly that season.

Something slammed that big ugly fly and my rod bucked. Line whirred off the shrieking reel. The trout jumped three times far away downstream. I looked in amazement as the backing flew off my reel. This had never happened before. I could see the nude metal on the revolving spool. I had just enough presence of mind to palm the reel at the last possible moment. The trout's insane run ended, and the furious tug-of-war began.

I can't say exactly how long it took me to land that trout. To this day, that Box Canyon fish remains my largest resident rainbow trout. I don't know exactly how large it was. Back then I didn't know how to measure a trout of that size accurately. I couldn't even begin to guess how much it weighed. I had no relevant experience to match it against. All I knew was that it took all the line and most of the backing off my reel in less than thirty seconds, and I must have spent fifteen minutes reviving it before I could safely release it back into the canyon.

I was to fish the Henry's Fork and the Firehole many times on that first autumn out West, and in the autumns and summers that followed. And I was to fish all of Cecil's rivers and more besides. And I would take all my vacations in the Yellowstone country. For a trout fisherman it is the Promised Land.

As a young man learning how to fly fish, I had been able to determine early on what so many others before me had already discovered: that the finest trout fishing in America was to be found in a rough circle around Yellowstone Park. Over the years I've lost faith in much, but never in that.

Four

DON'T FENCE ME IN

*W*inter doesn't leave Stanley, Idaho; it merely hovers a few thousand feet above town on the peaks of the Sawtooths. In summer the dormant snow remains visible up on the mountains, and you can almost feel winter waiting to sneak back down the slopes if given the opportunity.

Stanley Basin is what Sun Valley and Jackson Hole must have been like before they were discovered. I came to Stanley by a road that climbed over the mountains and immediately recognized that this former mining valley was far too good for tourism.

A huge thunderhead poured east ahead of me, spreading and darkening against the mountain range. The thunderhead slipped into the pass and the dark cloud split open, pouring rain onto cattle grazing below.

The basin's high meadow was blanketed with deep blue camas flowers. The upper Salmon River ran through the valley, and sparkling streams trickled out of the mountainsides. A hundred small lakes and beaver ponds remained hidden in the surrounding high country.

The tiny town of Stanley, with only ninety year-round residents, offered few commercial amenities, which suited me just fine. I wasn't prepared for the comfortable feeling I had in the presence of the townspeople, or of their log homes, wooden storefronts complete with hitching posts, and streets paved with God's clean dirt. Stanley looked like a lonesome stockade of rustic informality on a tranquil wilderness crossroads. The urge to drive on left completely.

I spent my first morning fishing for cutthroat trout in the Salmon River, which flowed through quiet ranch country where waterfowl summered and concealed themselves in the meadow grasses and along the irrigation ditches. The soft blue camas mantle and the placid Hereford cattle gave me a feeling of peace and pleasure before I ever wet a line. Sometimes I'd content myself by just sitting on the bank, legs dangling in the river, my bare head warm in the morning sunlight. I'd sniff the air, listen to the meadow, and ponder the mountains.

In the afternoon I might fish Yankee Fork where it flowed into the Salmon, or little Valley Creek if I found access through private ranchland. And there were brook trout to be tricked in high alpine lakes accessed by trails carpeted with lupines and blue columbines. The summer sun was warm at midday, but when it dropped behind the mountains the high country grew quite chilly.

As the sun set, everyone gathered at the Sawtooth Saloon or the Rod & Gun Club on unpaved Ace of Diamonds Street for the nightly "Stanley Stomp," an evening of dancing to live Western bands. The place jumped to cowboy violinists. The town, snug at the foot of the Sawtooths, maintained a kind of appearance of innocence that was almost touching.

Stanley Basin was considerably wilder back in the nineteenth century, when placer camps such as Hell Roaring, Bonanza, and Custer were going strong, filling up with the kinds of sterling characters that made the West great: get-rich schemers, squint-eyed gamblers, toothless muttering Gabby Hayes half-wits, demented women-hating hermits, McCabe-and-Mrs.-Miller brothel operators, dipso saloon keepers, and remittance men—those disgraced aristocrats sent west by their embarrassed families.

These were boom times in the mountains—before the veins of gold and silver petered out and a fire destroyed the largest of the placer camps. The slightly run-down valley soon shrank to its present-day population of honest, clean-necked citizens. It was almost impossible not to be utterly beguiled by Stanley's charming backwardness, what with the wind sighing in the pines and Eddie Arnold on the jukebox.

I spent a week in Stanley Basin; I wanted to spend years. All around me I saw routine Idaho magnificence. The upper Salmon was a ribbon of brightness in its meadow. That this peaceful headwater stream would transform itself downriver into the raging River of No Return was hard to believe.

The Salmon gathers from a maze of countless drainages in the Idaho mountains and runs for 425 mostly wilderness miles, the longest river contained within a single state. Its whitewater rapids carve through gorges before reaching the second deepest canyon in America, and it drains the largest roadless wilderness in the United States outside Alaska. And it's only a *tributary* to a tributary of the mighty Columbia River. The waters in Stanley Basin journey a long way toward their final mingling with the Pacific Ocean. Precisely how the Salmon River came to be known as the River of No Return is lost in the mists of Rocky Mountain legend, but I surmise it probably had to do with the fact that its whitewater currents were so powerful that upstream navigation was impossible until the invention of the jet boat. Once a raft or a supply barge was launched downriver, there was no going back. And yet here in its peaceful headwater meadows, the name *River of No Return* took on another meaning altogether.

A typical morning might begin at one of the campgrounds in the basin or in the old Sawtooth Hotel, if I had twenty dollars to splurge and wanted to enjoy a bath or a comfortable pine-board featherbed. Breakfast in the dining room was good honest fare, a stack of sourdough blueberry pancakes or a "Sawtooth egg"—a scrambled egg atop ham, cheese, and toast.

I would cross the meadow daily to a certain stretch of river I'd come to favor. Climbing the fence rail that blocked the path and straddling the top rail, I'd pause to gaze across the sun-drenched meadow carpeted in blue flowers. I'd take a moment to absorb the beauty of an unspoiled landscape and count myself among the most fortunate people on earth.

A picnic expedition took me to an alpine lake that remains nameless (I forgot the name), set almost eight thousand feet above sea level and surrounded by snowcapped peaks. As the trail led through pine forests and lush elk meadows, I remained alert for a glimpse of bighorn sheep. I caught pan-sized rainbow trout near the shoreline where a creek chilled by snowmelt emptied into the lake.

I contented myself with taking medium-sized trout out of the Salmon River. One afternoon another angler asked me if I'd seen steelhead in the river, a notion that shocked me. We were a thousand miles from the Pacific Ocean. He told me I should come out in March for the spring steelhead run, when the basin was still in the deep freeze of winter. The upper Salmon has great steelheading, he assured me, and fly rodders had an advantage in these clear shallow waters.

Each dawn I awoke to the snowcapped Sawtooths, with the White Cloud and Boulder mountains on the other side of the basin. The dawn light moved slowly over the peaks until the angle of sunlight caused the snowbank to erupt suddenly into a diamond brightness. *Ea dah how,* the native Shoshone called this land—literally "sun comes down the mountain" or "it is morning." All that is good and true seemed to be making its finest statement in these sparkling mountains and abundant streams.

Stanley would be a pretty good place to dig in for a last stand, I thought. Maybe build a log home here. Yes, a good plan, until I contemplated the nine-month winters with their piling snowdrifts and some of the coldest temperatures ever recorded in the lower forty-eight. Still, a small price to pay for a virgin valley and an untainted town.

How did I spend those days that slid by as easily as river water? I fished, naturally. But I listened, too, for birds and the music of wind on the mountains. The breezes passed through rocky crags humming like aeolian harps. Or issued from glens in a whisper of pines and shivering aspens. When thunderheads gathered, I counted lightning strikes on the granite peaks. I became an inspector of mayfly hatches. When the sun went down, I listened to the river running after it into the darkness. I luxuriated in splendid mountain isolation.

I lingered a while in Stanley. I like places where dogs still bury bones in the street. Towns like Stanley have not yet been discovered by the beautiful people. The mountain West still holds a few of these unknown snow bowls, and I was making it my duty to find them.

My road tour of the fishing West took me to Silver Creek, beckoning on the other side of the Sawtooths. Ketchum was an easy drive over the Galena Summit. The campground I had been staying at in Stanley Basin was no match for the ski lodges of Sun Valley.

Silver Creek was a startling piece of water. Here was a British chalkstream rising out of an alkaline desert. Hills as soft as chalk changed color slowly in the dry light.

The creek wends its way through an arid valley south of Ketchum. It's a large spring creek, slow moving, with meadow features. Its basin supports cattle ranches and potato farms. The valley is threaded by roads and irrigation sprinklers misting into alfalfa and barley fields. The cultivated bottomland grows out of a sagebrush landscape. It's an agricultural community bordering on a primitive desert. Dry bluffs and straw-colored hills rise above the cottonwoods behind Ketchum and Hailey.

Silver Creek seemed to me to spring magically from the flat arid landscape. Blackbirds perched and sang in tule thickets and from a forest of tall reeds along the banks. The creek's bed was thick with aquatic salad, nourished by springs on the bottom. The water was as clear as glass. The transparent bottom had been shaped in sweeping curves by the current's almost invisible but ceaseless motion. Emerald weeds waved and trailed in the glassy tongues of springwater. The submerged plants nurtured an abundance of delicate mayfly life.

I found the water astonishingly clean, its even, steady flow self-regulated by springheads barely affected by weather or drainage. Shoals of waterweeds showed near the surface as currents twisted their way through clusters of elodea and watercress.

The coiling, glassine surface of Silver Creek was as yet unbroken by any trout movement. Yet the rainbow trout were visible, outlined against a refracted bottom. They stood out most obviously against the streaming green plant life. The trout were shifting from side to side, intercepting mayflies still in their nymphal husks.

Before they take flight as diaphanous insects, mayflies live as nymphal swimmers on the stream bottom. Today's pupae struggling in their husks will be tomorrow's prolific hatches and mating swarms. The millions of mayflies that would emerge in the weeks and months to come were now living at the bottom of the stream. As with any trout stream, Silver Creek's insect life is far greater beneath the surface than above it.

Ernest Hemingway once shot ducks out of a canoe on this creek. Now this stretch of water is controlled and protected by The Nature Conservancy. I watched while softly gabbling mallards dipped their green heads into pond weed in backwater sloughs. Muskrat tunnels lined the undercut shoreline; herons had established rookeries back in the sloughs.

A V-shaped wake marked a big fish's route as it glided across a shallow patch of sandy bottom. Fish toured the surface, leaving sustained wakes as they moved about, swallowing insects before returning to their resting stations near the bottom.

As yet I hadn't seen any insects on the surface. But nymphs were floating upward toward the sunshine, struggling to break free of their husks. They would be vulnerable and helpless in the bewitching currents. The cruising rainbows were feeding on these emergers, taking them an inch or so below the surface.

I tied on an olive emerger and cast upstream with easy flicks of the wrist. The fly traveled back on a dead drift and I felt the electric twitch of a trout. The fish burrowed deeper into a bed of elodea. I ran my fingers down the vibrating leader, touching the trout. I was able to lift the fat trout out of the weeds and release it from the hook.

Yellow-green *Pseudocloeon* covered the water. Trout rose, bulging and dimpling the surface. The olive mayflies were drying their wings and taking flight. Rings spread and disappeared a little downstream of their rises. The trout were feeding steadily now. I tied on a very small Blue-Winged Olive and floated it downstream.

I heard low gurgling sounds, feeding plops. Trout had only to open their mouths to separate the insects from one medium to another. Smaller trout sucked the mayflies down noisily, gurgling at the take. Larger trout barely broke the surface tension in the film, sipping insects with little motion or effort.

This kind of fishing is as delicate a game as you can possibly imagine. I watched the feeding patterns of the trout and studied the vagaries of the current. My leader was made up of twelve feet of tapered monofilament pared down to an invisible hairline test of only two pounds' breaking strength. My tiny fly would slip downstream next to two or three naturals that trout were rising to. And when it all worked together it was magical.

The *Pseudocloeon* hatch lasted an hour or so. There was little motion on the creek's surface once the fluttering green flies had departed. Now and again a convulsive twitch might break the limpid water. A trout's position could be traced by a few simple bubbles as it rooted for nymphs on the bottom.

I heard the sky creak overhead. A great blue heron had taken leave. The heron's wings made a sound like a gate swinging open. The delicate bird disappeared behind the tule reeds.

I drove downriver to Point of Rocks. The lower creek was wider down there and the desert bottom a little more austere. The late-afternoon light made subtle changes on the smooth hills. Mayfly duns skittered and fluttered skyward. Half an hour later this hatch was followed by a mating swarm of small *Pseudocloeon*. The falling spinners triggered a decent rise. I hooked and released half a dozen trout, mostly browns. The Nature Conservancy water upstream was exclusively a rainbow trout fishery, but there were brown trout down by Point of Rocks, some going to eight pounds. The trout continued rising to *Pseudocloeon*. Hundreds of spent olive insects drifted past me in the currents among the elodea.

I fished out the evening, returning to the Conservancy water. The sky had turned to lavender. The hills around Silver Creek glowed sundown pink. It was exactly like the many photographs I had seen of Silver Creek in the fishing magazines. Once again, life was living up to its reputation.

I heard about Halfway, a forest and meadow town, set into a miniature version of the Rockies rising on an improbably green plateau in the high desert of eastern Oregon. My informant, one of those professional old-timers you always find occupying street benches and the booths in small-town coffee shops, clued me in to Halfway and the nearby town of Enterprise. He said that even though it was a kind of American Switzerland, not too many people knew about the Wallowa Valley. The plateau was topped by twin mountain ranges and the many lakes of the Eagle Cap Wilderness. This was the homeland from which Chief Joseph and his Nez Perce were exiled by the U.S. Cavalry, and to which he forever longed to return. Fly fishing could be had in virgin canyons of pine and sumptuous grassy meadows. The forks of the Lostine are filled with trout. The Imnaha River runs unmolested through log jams of fir, past cattle ranches and high pastures, finally spilling into a stunning canyon of whitewater before dropping into Hell's Canyon of the Snake River.

Of course, I was warned, if you go there, don't tell a soul . . .

One September, with the chroma of early autumn on the high country, I set out for Montana's Big Hole River. Here was ranch country not yet spoiled by tourism. I drove up from Idaho, watching orange-vested bird hunters setting out across the sagebrush desert around Arco. I followed the Red Rock River in Montana until it became the Beaverhead downstream of Clark Canyon Dam. I took a room in the small, friendly town of Dillon.

For me the very name Big Hole seemed to revoke the immensity of the Western landscape. Thousands of golden hay bales had been stacked up in the fields. Geese called down from the sky. I felt I had come to the very source of trout fishing in Montana.

I caught some large brown trout in the Big Hole below the town of Melrose. It surprised me that Big Hole trout were not at all leader shy. I could get by with heavy 2X and 1X leaders. Best of all, I took those slab-sized trout on a dry fly called a Joe's Hopper, which resembled the live grasshoppers sailing about in the meadow. The breezes blew the grasshoppers into the river, and the brown trout rose savagely to devour them. I knew things would continue like this until the first killer frosts of autumn came and wiped out the living grasshoppers.

Early the next morning I took a float on the willow-choked Beaverhead with a guide I had hired. At that time the Beaverhead had a reputation for surrendering the biggest brown trout in Montana. My guide's name was Chris. He told me he had been a philosophy major in college. "A discipline perfectly suited for rowing a boat all day," he explained.

The Beaverhead was very swift. And because of the thick bank willows, the Beaverhead was practically unwadable. I couldn't see much from the moving raft because of the wall of willow brush blocking the view of the surrounding ranch county. I cast flies tight against the brushy banks, as Chris had instructed. The river kept turning and twisting. I must have lost a dozen flies in those willows. Chris tried to cheer me up: "If you don't lose at least half a dozen flies in that brush," he said, "you can't really say you've fished the Beaverhead."

It had been very cold when we began in the early morning. Gradually the sun began to take the chill off the Beaverhead. I was hoping the change in temperature might stir the sluggish trout. And yet none of the river's vaunted brown trout came to my flies on that half-day float trip. Well, that's fishing.

The next day I headed north into the Bitterroot Mountains. I followed the trail of Chief Joseph and his fleeing Nez Perce. I walked the battlefield monument, the site where Colonel Gibbon's cavalry tried to massacre the sleeping Indians. The war chief

Looking Glass turned the battle around for the Nez Perce and Gibbon was badly wounded in the crotch, which proves there is a little justice in this world, but not much.

I fished the Bitterroot in its narrow mountain valley. I stayed in a fine little Montana town called Hamilton. I managed to find a copy of an out-of-print book I had been seeking, *John Medicine Wolf.* It was a kind of regional cult novel written by Michael Moon, a young Indian who lived in Hamilton.

I followed the Bitterroot down into Missoula, called "Meriwether" in James Crumley's detective novels. It was a university town with good bars. Outside Missoula, I fished Rock Creek in its timbered canyon. The cottonwoods and aspens along the stream had turned brilliant in the chilly autumn. Rock Creek's trout responded eagerly to my Elk Hair Caddis.

I drove eastward across Montana. The densely timbered high country gave way to sagebrush hills and lush cattle pastures. Shining mountain chains, rising out of the immense grasslands, stood miles apart, creating a sense of light and openness.

At Mallard's Rest on the Yellowstone River, the riffles sparkled in the sun. White shelving bars shined brightly under the blue-shadowed Absarokas. The cottonwood trees sheltering the banks were a brilliant flame of saffron. The Yellowstone divided here and there into braided channels.

I fished for brown trout as greenhead mallards drifted in the shallow backwaters or whirred overhead. I could feel the gravel slipping treacherously under my wading boots in the strong currents as I waded out from the shelving bars.

The autumn weather had stirred the brown trout, moving them onto their spawning beds. Brown trout are at their best in fall. I felt an electric hook-up and raised the rod. It was a heavy, powerful fish. I have come to believe that brown trout are stronger fighters than even rainbows, the famous aerialists; the mating urge makes browns more aggressive. Their colors had deepened and brightened in their autumn spawning regalia. The trout I landed on the Yellowstone River had taken on a glowing patina, like Italian Renaissance art.

The moving clouds and the light on the Absarokas seemed in tune with some great drama. The dusting of snow on the slate-colored peaks deepened the blue shadows along the range. Everything seemed meaningful and by design, as if these mountains were meant to teach us something about life.

I spent several days on the Yellowstone River fishing in sight of ranch buildings and cattle grazing in the broom-colored meadows. The foothills rose into greater ridges of dense pine forest, and then upward into the slate-gray serrations of the Absarokas.

Early one morning I followed the Yellowstone River up into Yankee Jim Canyon, through the Allenspar Notch, and then on to the high plateau of Yellowstone Park. I stopped briefly to gaze into the stunning ocher-rock gorge of the Grand Canyon of the Yellowstone. I continued on past the lushness and wildlife of the

Hayden Valley, where the wide, curving channels of the Yellowstone River were closed to fishing in the flat marshy meadows. I saw trumpeter swans on the river and a pair of moose along the banks. Plumes of white geyser steam erupted from the Mud Volcano area. I slowed the car to allow some bison to cross the road. The Yellowstone flowed flat and broad in the Sulphur Cauldron area. Soon I reached the lodgepole pines and meadow benches of Buffalo Ford.

Buffalo Ford is justifiably the most famous stretch on the Yellowstone. When the fishing season opens at Buffalo Ford in mid-July, it is always packed with fly fishermen. But by autumn the crowds can thin away to nothing. I counted only a handful of fly anglers at Buffalo Ford on this day. One of them was Cecil, the trout bum I had met on my first trip to the Yellowstone country.

The Yellowstone River at Buffalo Ford is very wide, ice cold, and deceptively smooth. Only a few miles upstream the river emerges from Yellowstone Lake as one of the largest trout streams in America. Its polished, deep glides pass over a clean gravel bottom. The Yellowstone in this smooth, glassy stretch is filled with the greatest concentration of native cutthroat trout on earth.

I said hello to Cecil. He was fishing a seam of current where trout were rising to tiny insects. I hadn't seen him since my first autumn in the Yellowstone country.

"They're rising to blue-winged olives," Cecil told me. He loaned me some of his flies, which were smaller than anything I had on me. We fished for about an hour, taking a good number of cutthroats between us. The cutts struggling on the ends of our lines showed olive and cranberry swirls under water. All the cutthroats at Buffalo Ford were uniformly large, sixteen to twenty inches in length.

"Is that a new rod?" I asked Cecil. He was fishing a honey-flamed bamboo rod. "Mind if I try it?"

"Okay. Break it, you bought it."

I forded the river so I could fish in the lee of the islands at midstream. The surface of the river appeared placid enough, but the current carried weight and authority. I felt gravel sliding away under my boots as I tried to wade the stream. But it was autumn and the Yellowstone River was low, so I was able to ford here without any mishaps.

A herd of bison on the opposite bank had spread out to graze over a rolling bench meadow the color of straw. When it comes to viewing wildlife, Yellowstone Park is an American Serengeti. The area is notorious for grizzlies, too, but the big bears aren't sociable and aren't often seen.

I heard bison on the move behind a screen of lodgepole pines directly across the river from me. The sound raised goose bumps. My hands were red and numb from handling so many trout in the icy water. I looked down at my feet; cutthroat trout finned in wavy reflections just inches from my boots. My ankles broke the flow of current and my boots doubtless were dislodging insect pupae from the gravel. The trout had deliberately positioned themselves in my wake.

Later that evening, after almost all the light had drained from the river, Cecil once again tried to teach me how to imitate the bugling of an elk in rut. "We'll see if we can call one down from the hills," he said.

The next morning I traveled to the broad valley of the Lamar River, a beautiful spot in the northeastern corner of the park that offered more good alpine scenery than any other place inside Yellowstone. The Lamar winds through broad sweeps of khaki grasslands that rise to clumps of scattered lodgepoles and eventually the snowcapped Absarokas. I stood by the river, not a soul in sight for miles. The Lamar bison herd grazed in the benchlands above me.

The valley had been scoured wide by a glacier, and now the Lamar River meandered back and forth rather aimlessly, creating marshes along its banks. Moose grazed in those wet depressions. The sagebrush slopes were dotted with islands of aspen; clumps of bright yellow balsamroot blanketed some of the arid hills.

I caught so many cutthroats in the sweeping bends of the Lamar River that I put off a trip to nearby Slough Creek and its three subalpine meadows for several days. I suspected that all the other anglers were there anyway. Slough Creek is famous for its meadow flats and slow-flowing pools that hold colorful cutthroat trout. But I had the Lamar River pretty much to myself.

One afternoon I was fishing little Soda Butte Creek, a clear-flowing tributary to the Lamar, and hail began pelting me from the sky. I continued to fish, taking half a dozen small cutthroats from the tumbling creek. Another day I hiked a few miles upstream where the Lamar River broke away from the road, at the junction of the Lamar and Soda Butte. The valley here looked like something out of the Pleistocene. A violent thunderstorm chased me out of the valley. The rain discolored the Lamar so badly that it became impossible to fish for days to come.

I took a room in the town of West Yellowstone. Quite often I would drive to the Gibbon River to fish at Gibbon Meadows and Elk Park. Elk grazed, mated, and gave birth in these meadows. It was autumn, so the bulls were gathering their harems. The elk looked magnificent in their sleek winter coats. The bulls were particularly impressive, with full spreads of antlers. The meadow rang with their bugling challenges. I could see the young bachelors without harems peering jealously from the screen of lodgepole pines fringing the meadows. In the evening one huge bull wapiti would come down to drink at Gibbon Meadows, stepping into the river very close to the spot where I was fishing. It was one of the great existential thrills of my life.

The Gibbon here was a typical western meadow stream with a sand-and-silt bottom. Its currents were easy; brown trout hid in protective undercuts along the banks. I'd catch these trout and release them back into the clear stream, then look across the meadow in the distance to see plumes of thermal steam rising from little Gibbon Geyser Basin, where Evening Primrose Spring, a deep, blossom-shaped crater filled with yellow mud, bubbled away.

The largest brown trout were to be found in the Madison River. These browns would move out of Montana's Hebgen Lake and swim upriver to spawn in the Madison inside Yellowstone Park. The travelers would swim all the way to Nine Mile Hole and even to the base of Firehole Falls. But the best place to fish for these spawners was in an area very close to the western boundary of the park, known locally as the Barns Pools or Behind the Barns.

Half a mile inside the park's West Entrance I turned onto a dirt road that took me to the Barns Pools, named after stables that once sheltered Yellowstone's horses and stagecoaches. At the end of the dirt road is a stretch of the Madison called Cable Car Run. The lower end of Cable Car is also known as Pool Number One. Around the bend downstream are two more holes, named—with an impressive lack of imagination—Number Two and Number Three. For the next three miles the Madison twists northwest in a series of oxbows toward the park's boundary. Many refer to this long stretch of the Madison as Beaver Meadows. Willow bogs and thick stands of lodgepole pine offer prime habitat for moose and grizzlies.

Late September through October is the time to fish the Barns holes and Beaver Meadows. Trout of up to four and five pounds swim up from Hebgen Lake and take shelter under the deep cuts in the meadows or rest in potholes along the rubble-strewn bottom. At any other time of the year, this stretch of the Madison is barren of anything but whitefish. But the bitter autumn season draws both the brown trout and the fly fishermen.

One afternoon under a leaden sky I hooked the largest brown trout I was to catch in Yellowstone Park. I caught it in Hole Number One; it took me a full ten minutes to land. I felt sure that the trout was going to escape and that I'd lose my prize. It flashed like brown and black gold under water. The fish I landed was deeply mottled, with warm butter-yellow shadings and black spots and a few as red as poppies.

Later that same afternoon, while fishing the quarter-mile bend of riffles between Holes One and Two, I took a huge rainbow trout where I least expected it. This rainbow turned out to be bigger than the brown I had landed earlier. An hour later, back in Hole Number One, I caught another large brown trout. It leapt out of the water, despite the fact that browns usually don't jump, and ran line off the reel in spurts. That day was a miracle.

I met a young man named Matt Stewart in West Yellowstone. He had taken a room at the Alpine Motel two doors down from me. The lady who owned the motel introduced us. She told me that Matt didn't know the high country and was looking for someone to fish with.

Matt had just driven in from North Carolina by way of Texas. He was a recent college grad; I think he said he majored in co-eds. He was enjoying a last fling before going into the family farming business back in North Carolina. On his way to Montana he had taken a slight detour to the Lone Star State to see a girl he had once met briefly on the off chance that something might come of it. Nothing did, so he headed for Yellowstone. Matt planned to spend a little time fishing for trout and then hunting birds up in the Canadian Rockies.

Matt and I fished the Firehole together, as well as a few other streams both in and out of the park. He was good company and very funny. He told me he had never seen anyone drink as much beer as I did, even back when he was in college. Every young person should have a role model.

After a few days of fishing in the park close by the roads, we decided we wanted to light out for the territory, so to speak. We weren't sure where to go. I suggested a long hike up into Pelican Creek, through the grizzly bear country north of Yellowstone Lake. But Bob Jacklin, the fly shop owner, told us that Pelican Creek was really only prime in early summer after the cutthroats had spawned. And so Matt and I selected as our destination the Bechler River in the hard-to-reach southwestern corner of Yellowstone Park.

To reach the Bechler Wilderness, we had to leave West Yellowstone and drive all the way over Targhee Pass into Idaho. Matt and

I followed the Henry's Fork of the Snake River until we got to the dusty town of Ashton, and then we turned back toward the northeast, reentering Yellowstone Park at its remote Idaho entrance. The road into the pines turned to gravel and dust. A ranger at the old soldier station—a relic of those times when the U.S. Cavalry rode the boundary trails, keeping poachers and (worse) cattle out of the park—told us that five-pound rainbows hiding under the meadow banks of the Bechler River would slash out hungrily for our Joe's Hoppers. Matt saw me stashing cans of Coors into my backpack. My plan was to chill them later in the Bechler River.

We hiked across the meadows and through the pines for three miles until we arrived at Bechler Meadows. We didn't need any insect repellent because it was late in the season and the marshy meadows had dried out. We wouldn't be plagued with any biting blackflies or mosquitoes. The Bechler meandered rather aimlessly in a four-mile-long stretch of meadow, its banks lined by willow bushes. Few trees obstructed our view of the meadow river. The water was like purest vodka, with clear pools, undercut banks, and overhanging grasses, and the scene put me in mind of photographs I had seen of New Zealand trout rivers. The rainbow trout tended to hold at midstream, wide open and exposed in very clear water. The pools were so transparent that it was like looking at the river bottom through a lens.

"You could read the *New York Times* in this water," I told Matt. I raised my rod tip and sent a rainbow trout bolting for cover.

"We're going to have to crawl on our hands and knees just to get near these fish," said Matt. The extreme clarity made everything on the bottom visible. A few very large trout had taken up widely scattered positions in the stream. One cast apiece was about all we'd get to these trout.

We spooked almost every fish we cast to. And on those rare occasions when the trout weren't scurrying for cover, they simply ignored our Joe's Hoppers. Finally Matt and I threaded live hoppers onto hooks that we had stripped bare. This was grossly illegal; bait fishing is banned in most of Yellowstone Park. But we figured, what the hell, we were going to let the trout go anyway.

Finally a big rainbow, or perhaps it was a rainbow-cutthroat hybrid, rose and seized Matt's live, kicking grasshopper. The water exploded and boiled as the trout thrashed for its life. Matt managed to horse the heavy, struggling fish over to the bank, but when he reached down to capture his prize, the trout exploded in a second wind and the hook came free. Matt almost fell into the river trying to grab that fish before it fled downstream. I couldn't stop laughing.

Driving back in the darkness, after the long hike out of Bechler Meadows, I almost ran into a cow that had strayed onto the highway from the unfenced Idaho cattle pastures. Cattle were all over the highway, all around us, their stupid bovine faces lit up by moonlight.

On Matt's last day at Yellowstone the two of us fished the Firehole River. I took him to Fountain Flats. The river was empty of fishermen, and the basin had filled with what must have been 100 to 150 bison. Trout were sipping tiny *Pseudocloeon* flies. We rummaged in our fly boxes for something small enough to imitate the greenish spinners. The river was pockmarked with disappearing trout rings.

We fished throughout a long afternoon under a stormy sky. A low front had descended over the Rocky Mountains. The storm had dropped a foot of snow on Sun Valley the night before, and now dark squall lines were moving in on the Yellowstone Plateau. But we didn't want to leave the Firehole. The stream was actually warmer than the air around us. And the pull of current, the soothing effect of running water, lulled our senses into a state of contentment.

I want to remember that day as it was. The Firehole trout rising to the spinner fall. The bison gathered in the meadow. Steam escaping the geysers, and the snow about to fall. And most of all, the stillness.

Things change. When I first visited Stanley Basin, I vowed to keep the place a secret from all but my closest fishing friends. I needn't have bothered. Instead I should have sunk all the money I had into Stanley real estate. Likewise with the Wallowa Valley in Oregon.

Even back in those days Silver Creek, Sun Valley, and Ketchum were well outside my income bracket. Today living in or around Sun Valley would be entirely out of the question.

Tourism has gradually come to the beautiful valley of the Big Hole. And along the lovely Bitterroot lie many retirement homes and much private property.

The spacious ranchland in Paradise Valley that borders the Yellowstone River under the Absarokas is being subdivided for future housing development. So too is the ranchland along Montana's Madison River outside Yellowstone Park.

More fly fishermen than ever before are visiting Yellowstone. Autumn is no longer the solitary season it once was.

Five

GOOD-BYE TO ALL THAT

*I*n the spring of 1988 I quit my newspaper job. My plan was simple—I would take an entire year off and bum around the American West, fishing my brains out. I believe it was David Hume who said something to the effect that reason is slave to our passions.

My plan, if you want to call it a plan, was to move out West permanently. But beyond that I really hadn't decided where I would finally end up. I would play it by ear. I think the idea essentially was to start life over, whatever that means.

I had been contemplating moving out West for some time. I'd had it with the East Coast. I had a good job there, but I wanted to live out West—partly in order to be able to fish more often, but mostly for a necessary change of scene, and in order to refresh the senses and the spirit. The West was the place to go. Living where

I lived, I could only manage three or four good weeks of trout fishing out West a year, and I wanted more. Fly fishing meant so much to me, it only seemed reasonable to move out there.

But before I took another job or decided on a place to relocate, I wanted to fulfill a long-standing dream. That dream was to take an entire summer, or maybe even an entire year off, if need be, just to travel all over the western United States fly fishing. I thought of it as a kind of grand tour of trout fishing in America, or at least the best part of America. Afterward, once I'd gotten this out of my system, I would find a place I liked out West, settle in, and resume my interrupted career. I knew I had the journalistic and writing skills to make a good living anywhere I decided to resettle. And I had been saving up my money for such an adventure.

I should point out that I wasn't married, so I could pull off a stunt like this. I had no commitments, no binding ties, nothing holding me back. I had never done anything remotely like it before, either. As an adult, I had never been without a job. And now I was about to end a fifteen-year career at my newspaper to go fishing all the doo-dah day.

Part of my motivation must have come from the fact that I began reporting for the newspaper while I was still in college, as a student intern, working part-time during the school year and full- time in summer, and so I never took off for a summer of backpacking in Europe or completed any of those other rites of passage that young people undertake at a certain time in their lives. I was instead moving about in the adult world practicing journalism—and having quite a ball at it, I might add. Upon my graduation from college, my paper hired me full-time, and I'd been there ever since. So I could look at my western fishing trip as a youthful lark deferred until middle age.

My other motivation was that I had become bored with my job. The route I had taken as a newspaperman began somewhat typically with the writing of obituaries and news features and covering town meetings, but—because this was Atlantic City—my job soon expanded into exposing crooked politicians and probing Mafia activity around the periphery of the casino gambling industry. Before I knew it I had become the newspaper's investigative reporter. It was all highly entertaining, as addictive as eating potato chips, and about as nutritious. In time, even covering the comic-book exploits of a mob that couldn't shoot straight (but straight enough, with two dozen murders and still counting) became a bit of a predictable routine, and I felt that I was growing stale. I might have been relieving my readership of some of its day-to-day tedium, but I was doing little to free myself from the tyranny of my own dull mind.

Many newspaper reporters daydreamed about becoming serious writers. I had found it too easy to be seduced by the pleasures of daily journalism, the ready-made audience for a good story, and the instantaneous acclaim for a scoop. My newspaper work demanded little from me in the way of excellence in writing beyond speed, clarity, and accuracy. Those were good disciplines, but I knew there was more to good writing. There was certainly more to creating literature. No newspaper reporter could expect his words to last, I knew that. Words appearing in newsprint survived about as long as the lifespan of an adult mayfly. Novels, autobiography, memoir, essays—those were another matter.

And so I'd gotten the half-assed idea that my trip just might help me become a better writer. I wanted to explore that part of the world that wasn't in the headlines. You learn about life not just through books but also through action, and journalism perhaps provides a little of the kind of experience you can't get elsewhere without going to war. But in both war and journalism, the goal is to get out alive, preferably with your sanity. I saw fishing as another form of action and experience, a way of exploring the deeper, physical world we inhabit, that world we have come to call, for want of a better term, the natural world.

The natural world was pretty much finished in New Jersey anyway. The death of nature in the ironically named Garden State had created a spiritual void in my life. Casino gambling had brought with it an unprecedented development boom throughout all of southern New Jersey, and places like the Pine Barrens, nature's last stronghold in the most densely populated state in the Union, were feeling the pressure. I would come back from my Western fly-fishing vacations refreshed in body and spirit—only to find myself deeply saddened and even depressed by what I was returning to. One summer I came back from vacation to find dead dolphins awash on the beaches, a witch's brew of chemical pollutants in the ocean, New York City's garbage floating on the tide, and a pall of carbon-monoxide poison hanging over the Pine Barrens.

At the time I lived in a house on a seven-acre patch of pines and blackjack oaks in a small rural township called Estell Manor. It was only a short drive from the shore. I might drive out from my home—say, on a late-spring day—and, crossing the Tuckahoe River, notice the cattail marshes at dead low tide, mallard ducks feeding in the shallows. Red-winged blackbirds flitted in and out of the reeds. No doubt there were striped bass all the way up the creeks. Here the land was at its lowest, the tidal creeks draining sluggishly toward the bay. Looking at a tidal marsh, my emotions ran higher, my sense of well-being quickened, and I became closer to my true self.

More blackjack oaks, and then abruptly the trees gave way to the panorama of green marsh grass. Straight ahead a tall bridge rose steeply above a blue bay and emerald plain. Here, between the mainland and the barrier island, the sky began to take on the feeling of openness that comes near the ocean.

Liquor stores and motels lined the causeway to the island, but the salt meadow that lay beyond was as green as the fairway on a country club. The mudflats, more nutritious than the greenest Iowa cornfield, lay exposed by an outgoing tide. I spotted flounder holes and a gut where bluefish passed in schools. The barrier island seemed to be held in place by jetties, seawalls, and breakers. I liked to tell myself that the development boom along the coast couldn't last—that someday a hurricane would blow it all away. But I knew that profit and commerce and a flood of cash and high times would keep nature at bay. Those condominiums, marinas, and glass beach houses weren't going away anytime soon. They could all be rebuilt after a hurricane, bigger and shinier than ever. Scientists say life began at the seashore; now there was a serious question whether life could continue there.

New Jersey was a place I could take only so much of, and I knew I couldn't take it at all without the shore and the Pine Barrens. I used to frequent a tavern called the Green Bank Inn on the Mullica River, in the heart of the Pine Barrens. It was my favorite bar, located near a small backwater called Batsto, a historical Pine Barrens town that operated as a tourist trap. The inn, a great beer joint, used to be a crossroads jug tavern and was haunted by the ghost of a Revolutionary War soldier. I wrote a feature on the bar and the ghost for my newspaper.

On weekends in May, my friends and I would stock up on cold beer at the Green Bank Inn and then go canoeing on nearby rivers like the Mullica and the Wading. The rivers were always crowded—May is the prime month for canoeing in the Pine Barrens. It wasn't the Adirondacks by any means, but the rivers of the Pine Barrens had their own special charm.

The afternoon light filtering down on the riverbanks was green and diffused, like the shade under a beach umbrella. The river, no more than fifteen feet across in most places, was the color of strong tea; the water had a cool vegetable odor under the trees. Our canoes slid easily along, turning and twisting with the river beneath a dense canopy of Atlantic white cedar and box elder. I would stare down into the passing dimness of the river bottom as painted box turtles slid off their logs and splashed into the water at our approach.

Because this was cedar water, the river was dark, almost opaque. Tannins from the cedars leached out of the ground, mixing with iron, giving the rivers that dark, tealike color. In my childhood you could drink straight from Pine Barrens rivers. Pine Barrens water stayed fresher longer than any other available water, and sea captains stored it in barrels for long voyages. The rivers originated in the pine forests and emptied into either the ocean or Delaware Bay. In the past the water had been potable because there was no industry in the woods to pollute the creeks and rivers. But the water was no longer truly safe to drink; there were too many blueberry and cranberry farms and septic tanks out there now.

Every elbow turn on the river brought on much the same view of the woods. The cedars and box elders lining the banks were so dense that I could hardly see past the foliage, and I felt pleasantly cut off from the world. A bend at the bank on our right rose up slightly higher and we broke out of the river shade into brilliant sunshine. A mountain of trash bags had been piled onto the bank, and the air stank. Beyond this trash pile there was a wide clearing, a large swath cut out of the pines and blackjack oaks, and a sand road that cut through a spong, or low area in the woods, full of high-bush blueberry that ended at a fingerboard in the pines, a place where several sand roads all came together. There was a garbage strike under way in Philadelphia, and word had gotten out among some city residents that they could drive out to the New Jersey Pine Barrens and find convenient places to dump their trash, mainly along the sand roads and the riverbanks. As we canoed along for the next several miles we counted innumerable trash bags stacked up along the river. You never love a place so much as when you're in danger of losing it.

One day I drove deep into the pinelands to write a story about a tiny hamlet called Mullica Township, a charming backwater, the Athens of South Jersey. I nosed around for a few days and discovered that the mayor had built an extension onto his house without first bothering to obtain a building permit. One committeeman, perhaps the township's dumbest, had built an entire three-story house without having obtained a single building permit and was storing heavy construction machinery on land zoned for residential use. Another committeeman had trespassed on state tidal land by illegally building a floating dock off his home on the Mullica River. And the town clerk had put up a new roof on his general store without a permit—besides having maintained a junkyard on his property for years without any mercantile license. The Pine Barrens didn't seem to mean anything special to these people. Maybe that was the problem: No place is special to people who've lived there all their lives.

I spent a day in the Pine Barrens driving around the sand roads with a New Jersey state trooper on the lookout for human mischief. The trooper wanted me to see a dumpsite for stolen vehicles that was favored by hoodlums. We passed by a cranberry farm divided by low dikes that crisscrossed a bright green mat of plants. A blue reservoir pond reflected an unblemished sky. The bogs were all drained and would not be flooded until the autumn harvest. Cranberries and blueberries were the only crops under cultivation in the Pine Barrens because the soil was too sandy and acidic for any other kind of farming. It was a little too early in the season for blossom time, when the farmers would bring in bees to pollinate the vines. Bees didn't care much for cranberry blossoms, preferring to fly off into the woods in search of wildflowers. So the farmers had to bring in extra hives. The pinkish blossoms resembled crane's heads, which is how cranberries got their name. The unripe berries were white and wouldn't turn crimson until fall. Only the swamps of Cape Cod and the boglands of Wisconsin produced more cranberries than the New Jersey Pine Barrens.

The deep woods were full of bog asphodel, swamp hyacinth, dogbane, clusters of a bright little flower known as sandwort, which Pineys call sparkle, and a jungle of sheep laurel. There were twenty-three kinds of orchids growing in the woods, inclding the delicate orchid known as a lady's slipper; Pineys call it a "whoppoorwill shoe." But most interesting of all were the flesh-eating plants, like the thread-leaved sundew that trapped insects in its spine-covered leaves. These rare, carnivorous plants had adapted to the nitrogen-poor soil of the Pine Barrens by getting their nitrogen from insects they captured and digested. We passed tarpaper shacks and the occasional saltbox house hidden away behind acres of pine, blackjack oak, and high-bush blueberry. It's easy to get lost in the Pine Barrens, even though you're never more than a few miles from a road. Forest rangers are forever pulling out lost deer hunters and Boy Scouts. They get turned around in the bracken and start walking in circles. You can orient yourself by the trees, however. The pitch pines, which Pineys called bull pines, grow on higher, dry ground. Taller Atlantic cedars are found growing in cripples, low-lying ground alongside riverbanks. There's even a plain of dwarf pines where, simply standing, you can look out over the heads of the trees and see for miles.

We descended into a wallow, a quaking bog, and the sphagnum moss, which absorbs tremendous amounts of water, made the ground feel like it was shaking under us. Then we came upon a clearing littered with the burned-out frame of an abandoned car. The pinelands were favored as a convenient burial ground for mob hits as well as a handy place to abandon a torched automobile. Historically the Pine Barrens have always been a hideout for highwaymen and moonshiners, deserting Hessians, and Quakers who couldn't live up to moral codes. The sand roads attract suicides and murders. There's no telling how many bodies lie in unmarked graves in these woods. The Pine Barrens might be unlike anyplace else in the eastern United States, more remarkable than most people could even guess, but to the people who live out here or who come into the woods to commit their crimes, they're just part of regular life.

For a time I was attracted to fishing the mysterious cedar waters of the Pine Barrens. The tannic lakes and streams were filled with small, toothy pickerel, but this kind of fishing really wasn't very interesting. Still, it was always a privilege to come to these woods with their vanished towns, iron bogs, and wallows. It was a hidden world back there in the pines, and it was hard to believe that it had held off the onslaught of civilization for so long. Much of the area was state owned and preserved. But developers were gnawing away at the edges, throwing up housing developments where the only pine scent presumably would come out of an aerosol can.

For about ten years part of my routine had been to fly fish in the ocean. Because the trout fishing in New Jersey was so mediocre, I turned to the sea. Funny, but for all those years I was fly fishing in the ocean for striped bass and bluefish, I never once saw another fly angler on the beach. I had the impression I was the only one who was doing it, and although I knew that couldn't possibly be the case, it made me feel a little like some kind of fly-fishing pioneer.

Even when it's calm, the surf makes a breathing sound. On an island you hear it all around you even if you can't see the water. I had driven out to Corson's Inlet, at the extreme southern tip of the barrier island known as Ocean City, and parked my car behind the dunes. I could hear the suspiration of the ocean on the other side of the dunes.

I assembled my fly rod and struck out on a well-worn path through the dunes. The backdunes were bursting with goldenrod and sea rocket; I swatted at greenheads buzzing around my face. The New Jersey state bird is the mosquito, but in the sand dunes it's the greenheads that eat you alive. Climbing out at last over the ridge of primary dunes, I saw the Atlantic combers rolling in. The surf crunched and hissed against the sand, and as I walked along the waterline, the wet sand squeaked under my bare feet. I headed south toward the huge sandspit at the very end of the island, where the incoming tide raced over Corson's Inlet, over shallow sandbars and deeper trenches. Across the inlet lay Strathmere, another resort island.

I looked for wheeling gulls over the water. Their presence often indicates a school of bluefish crashing bait. I didn't see any working gulls, but I did spot a four-wheel-drive jeep at the end of the sandspit and an official-looking person bending over something by the water's edge. As I drew closer, I could see that the inert form on the beach was a dead Atlantic bottlenose dolphin. A uniformed woman knelt beside the dolphin and was drawing blood into a syringe. A bad sign.

The previous summer, the Atlantic had brought up a noxious cargo of medical waste, bloody gauze, dirty hypodermic needles, and scores of dead dolphins. Something was killing the dolphins along the Jersey shore—and in the Mediterranean, the North Sea, and the Gulf of Mexico, too. Most of the theories about why dolphins were perishing had to do with pollution. In New Jersey the chief suspect was the New York Bight: Currents were sending garbage dumped into the bight down to the Jersey shore. Blood tests on the dead dolphins showed a link to Morbillivirus, from the same family of diseases that cause measles and canine distemper. Something, probably pollutants, had compromised and weakened the immune systems of dolphins and seals, causing them to succumb to the virus.

The woman finished drawing blood and then placed her syringes and specimen bags into a metal box. A man helped her lift the dead dolphin into the back of the jeep. The dolphin's skin looked like wet neoprene. I noticed nearby sanderlings foraging at the waterline, chasing the retreating foam. Shorebirds seem to make the beach move, and I couldn't help but wonder what the beach would be like without their movement.

Across the beach a heavyset man burdened with a television video camera struggled over a foredune. By now the dead dolphin had drawn a small crowd. A collie straining at its leash barked incessantly at the inert form in the back of the jeep, sealed in its gray neoprene skin. The overweight newsman with the video camera stumbled his way across the sand to get footage for the evening news.

In Peru, people eat dolphin. It's a popular dish served in seaside cafés. Locals call the dish *muchame,* "sea pig." The meat is taken from the dorsal muscle, salted, and hung to dry like oversized beef jerky. Italian immigrants from Genoa who settled on the coast introduced sea pig to the Peruvians. A little garlic, olive oil, and sliced avocado is all it really needs.

Now maybe this was a solution to New Jersey's dolphin problem: Open up a string of clam shacks on the beach and sell *muchame* to the tourists. I was more than ready to give up this scene. And I figured it was now or never.

Basic human impulses conflict with living a good life, and we must all live with our conflicting desires. People talk about getting in touch with their feelings, as if that's always a positive thing. But there's danger in it, too. You just might find yourself without a job.

I told very few people in advance about my plans to give up the uncreative, dead-end life I felt I was leading. Certainly I told no one at my newspaper, not until the day I formally announced my resignation. I had no idea what my colleagues' reaction might be—probably incredulity. I felt a little incredulous myself. Imagine giving up a job to go trout fishing! I was either the bravest man on earth or the most foolish. I hadn't quite made up my mind which. But I felt the trip was something I just had to do. I wanted to get away badly. I wanted to explore the wilder and better parts of America and the deeper parts of myself. And I wanted the satisfaction of being able to tell myself that I had the guts to make the break.

About a month before I finally pulled up stakes, I found myself having lunch in a Philadelphia restaurant during a break in a Mafia trial with a private detective named Alan Hart. Alan was lending his investigative talents to the defense lawyers, who were working very hard on behalf of an Atlantic City mob boss charged with ordering a gangland murder in the City of Brotherly Love. That morning Alan had managed to demolish the credibility of the prosecution's chief witness in the case, a mobster who had turned informant, and who had testified in great detail about a phone call he purportedly made from a phone booth on a street corner in Philadelphia that had triggered a Mafia hit. Alan proved through phone company records that no public phone booth had ever existed at the location mentioned by the Mafia turncoat. You didn't get to see that many Perry Mason moments in a courtroom. It was one of the things I was going to miss. Over lunch, I casually mentioned to Alan that I had tendered my resignation and was headed out West to take a fly-fishing trip of indeterminate length; I wouldn't be back. Alan looked at me in amazement.

"You're my hero," he said.

And so after wrapping up that final Mafia trial—just one in a series of many that I had covered, so many that they all had begun to blur into one endless and, I thought, rather pointless and protracted Mafia farce—I made my preparations to hit the road. I put my belongings into storage (to be sent for later after I resettled, wherever that might be) and filled my car with fishing and camping gear. I had two things going in my favor: I had more money in my bank account than Jack Keruoac and William Least Heat Moon had when they hit the road; and I weighed much less than Charles Kuralt.

Yellowstone Park seemed the likely place to start my adventure.

Six

THE SUMMER OF LIVING DANGEROUSLY

I arrived in West Yellowstone on the final day of June. The weather was unseasonably warm, the air unusually dry, but to me the high plateau looked as glorious and inviting as I'd ever seen it. West Yellowstone was one of the few places where I felt completely comfortable, one of the places I could go to to be truly happy.

I noticed a thin column of smoke in the distance hanging like a pale blue apparition. No doubt smoke from a small forest fire. It seemed to be coming out of the northeastern part of the park, or just beyond it. Forest fires are common in summertime, nothing to worry about, and the National Park Service generally leaves them alone to burn.

Looking over my journal entries from this period, it is remarkable how satisfied I felt having arrived here. Here are some edited entries from that journal:

June 30

I arrived in West Yellowstone after four days on the road, having quit the only job I've ever had. I was feeling a little bit apprehensive as I hit the road. But when I arrived in West Yellowstone at 2:30 P.M., driving up in the morning from Rock Springs—suddenly, I had a great feeling of release. How good to be back in Yellowstone Park again. All feelings of apprehension have lifted away.

The guys at Bud Lilly's fly shop said the Gallatin both inside and outside the park was hot. It seemed a good place to begin my fishing. The weather was warm, the day brilliant. I fished caddis on the Gallatin, right below where the Taylor's Fork comes in, just outside the park. Landed a rainbow, about twelve inches—lost a bigger one. Missed about half a dozen strikes. Guess I'm rusty.

There was a great evening caddis hatch on the Madison River. The sun sank behind the mountains, putting the river in shadow. I had driven back to West Yellowstone for dinner, and later I went out on the Madison, behind the Barns. The caddis hatch was right on schedule. Fish were rising everywhere in the river. Unfortunately they were all whitefish. I must have caught about twenty whitefish and one very small brown trout. There is a saying among Western fly fishermen that no one ever caught a whitefish on purpose. What the hell, I guess I'm just an eastern rube. These were big whitefish. The sunset was deep, the light clear. The river was low from the dry weather.

July 1

I fished the Henry's Fork on the Harriman Ranch. The day was brilliant and hot, and very dry. Got to the water about midafternoon. No rises, just some PMDs floating by every once in a while. I had only one strike. The wind started blowing pretty hard around 3 P.M., so I hung it up and walked back across the meadow. Only one other angler on the water, and he had done nothing.

I drove back past Henry's Lake, stopping briefly to fish Grayling Creek. The water ran over small stones, past brushy willow banks. A pretty little stream. I caught a few small rainbows.

Later that evening I fished the Madison at Grasshopper Bank. I lost the first fish I struck during the caddis hatch, and landed two whitefish. I was probably making a mistake by fishing the Madison at this time of the season, but the river's so lovely, and the evening deep and clear.

No regrets about leaving my job and coming out here. This is the life I was born for.

July 2

Spent the early morning and afternoon on the Gallatin. It was a beautiful, clear day and the fishing was excellent. There were no hatches, but I landed five rainbows on an Elk Hair Caddis. I fished the stretch below the Taylor's Fork—the long, flat stretch. Afterward I went to Grayling Creek above the highway bridge, just below Tepee Creek. I was probably just in and just out of the park. I landed a few small rainbows hiding under a sunken log, and I missed lots of rises to small fish as I worked my way upstream.

Later that evening I went back to the Madison. My first stop was at that small bench meadow just above Nine-Mile Hole. There was a flotilla of caddis on the water, a regatta of duns. But not a single rise on the smooth water. I left the bench meadow for the Barns near the park boundary, where I landed a small brown trout and lots of annoying whitefish.

July 3

I fished the Madison outside the park across from the Morgan Ranch. I took five brown trout, losing a big one near the bank. It was hard fishing, with the wind howling down the Madison Valley. I was fishing a caddis dry. I took a little satisfaction in the fact that most of the other anglers weren't doing much of anything. I must be doing something right.

That evening I went back to the Madison in the park and fished Grasshopper Bank. Took only large whitefish in the slow deep water. And then I went back behind the Barns and caught more whitefish in a blizzard of a caddis hatch. I fished until dark, at 10 P.M. I love summer twilights at this latitude.

July 4

Fourth of July. I walked the Ranch waters on the Henry's Fork, all the way around Big Bend. Lots of wind on that long walk; sunny and high clouds. Man, the weather is really dry. Didn't see a single rise on the water. Didn't even wet my line.

Drove over to the Madison at the Slide area just below Quake Lake. What an ugly piece of water; this place is a real eyesore. But oh man, are there huge trout in this stretch! I lost a humongous rainbow in one of the fast chutes. It really put a bend in my rod. Saw another fellow land a really chunky brown. Left around 4 P.M. when a sudden thunderstorm covered the ground in hailstones.

July 5

I plucked eight brown trout out of Gibbon Meadows. There were no insects hatching that evening; I was expecting a hatch of brown drakes. I took all the fish on an Elk Hair Caddis. What a gorgeous, peaceful meadow. My biggest fish was fifteen inches.

Earlier in the day I had to drive the 175-mile round trip to Bozeman, to get my prescription polarized sunglasses fixed; I had broken the wire rim. I fished the Gallatin on the way back, but it was very windy. The evening fishing on the Gibbon River was sweet anodyne and made up for the rotten start to the day.

July 6

Fished the Gallatin inside the park in the late morning. I landed two cutthroats, the first a fifteen-inch beauty with a remarkable slash of color on its throat. I had not fished more than forty-five minutes before a brief rain shower chased me away. The rain didn't last; barely moistened the dusty ground.

Later that evening, after the weather cleared up, I returned to Gibbon Meadows, but I didn't repeat my success of the previous evening. I saw a few brown drakes coming off the water. These mayflies are said to favor the silty bottoms of the Gibbon in the slow currents of Elk Park and Gibbon Meadows. I lost a small brown trout, and missed a few strikes, and that was it.

July 7

I fished the Lamar River in its sweeping valley. I landed seven cutthroats. I took the majority of them at a favorite bank where I had some stunning success last summer. The cutthroat in the Lamar had a reputation for cruising around and never staying in one place. But I had taken cutts off that bank time and time again. The biggest trout I landed was twenty inches—a remarkable fish, the equal of the big cutthroats found at Buffalo Ford on the Yellowstone.

The sun was high, the weather pleasant and not too breezy. Bison grazed in the meadow benches of the Lamar Valley. Later I fished Slough Creek, hooking a cutthroat but losing it because I hauled back too hard. I fished the meadow water of Slough Creek below the campground. Plan to hike up to one of its higher meadows tomorrow.

July 8

What is the attraction of Slough Creek? Hiked in to the First Meadow and found the fishing mediocre. Pretty place, though. I fished for a while without catching anything and then hiked back out as quickly as I could. Lots of annoying, biting blackflies up here.

I spent the remainder of the day on the Lamar, taking cutthroat after cutthroat out of the grassy, undercut banks. I've always had better luck on the Lamar than on Slough Creek, for some reason. I caught a few cutts that went sixteen and seventeen inches. Very satisfactory. The weather was sunny and very hot.

JULY 9

I caught a big rainbow on the Madison today. Slammed the car door on my Scott rod and broke the tip off earlier in the day when I was on the Gallatin. Took it over to Blue Ribbon Flies in West Yellowstone to be repaired. I'm fishing with my backup rod, a real piece of crap. Hope I get my old rod back soon. They promised it in a couple of days.

JULY 10

I landed eight trout and one whitefish on the Gallatin inside the park. The largest was a rainbow of fifteen inches. Most averaged twelve to fourteen inches and were either rainbows or rainbow-cutthroat hybrids. I was fishing a caddis as usual, and then switched to a PMD. The day was a bit overcast, but parched. When the wind died down, the biting blackflies were atrocious.

July 11

I landed fifteen brook trout—four to eleven inches apiece—on the upper Gardner River below Sheepeater Cliffs. Lord, these are the prettiest brookies I've ever seen. So sleek and beautiful, their colors a deep violet cast. They jumped all over my caddis. This is a really wild and beautiful spot. And no other fishermen around.

July 12

I fished the Gallatin in the park again. It was overcast and windy, but there was no rain. We could use some. I pulled a few trout and whitefish out of the water.

In the late afternoon I drove seventy miles to check out the lower Madison below the town of Ennis. I took only one rainbow, on a weighted nymph. There was a spectacular golden sunset on the way back to West Yellowstone. The Madison River and its mountain ranges appeared quite stunning in this light, which seemed to be passing through a hazy filter that came from the smoke emanating from a handful of small forest fires burning inside the park.

JULY 13

I drove to Paradise Valley to fish the Yellowstone at Mallard's Rest. The day was hot, dry, and terribly windy. The riffles glittered and the shelving bars shined in the sun. I fished drys and nymphs and caught some trout under the blue-shadowed Absaroka Mountains.

JULY 14

I took four or five cutthroats and rainbows on the Gallatin. I also lost two good ones. My best landed was fourteen or fifteen inches. The two I lost felt bigger. I took all the fish on dry flies inside the park. The day was sunny and dry, and pretty windy.

JULY 15

Opening day on the Yellowstone River at Buffalo Ford in the park. But no easy success like last year. Here I was, standing in the midst of the greatest concentration of cutthroat trout on the planet, and it was all I could do to land one big fish. It was sunny and hot in the lodgepole basin. There are forest fires still burning within the park. The fires are growing. The radio is reporting that this is the driest summer in Yellowstone Park's 112-year history.

Naturally, fishing pressure was quite heavy on opening day at Buffalo Ford. But it's always worth coming out here. The Yellowstone is very accessible in this stretch below Fishing Bridge and the Mud Volcano. There are miles and miles of cutthroat trout on the gravel bottoms, and the Yellowstone passing through the dark lodgepole forest is stunningly beautiful.

JULY 16

A better day at Buffalo Ford. I fished in the lee of the islands, my favorite spot. Sunny and hot just like yesterday. But there were good insect hatches and lots of rising trout. The Yellowstone flows out of the nation's largest alpine lake and is a virtual trout factory.

JULY 17

Fished the Yellowstone below Buffalo Ford again. A wonderful day. I got there late, around 1 P.M. The fishing was slow at first. And then the caddis started coming off in the soft evening light. It was a wonderful rise. I landed ten fish, all long, heavy trout, between seventeen and twenty inches. A few of my flies popped off;

I was fishing a very light leader. It was a gorgeous and completely satisfactory evening. I left the river around 7:45 P.M. Maybe my best day thus far this summer.

July 18

A hypnotic evening dry-fly fishing on the Yellowstone at Buffalo Ford. I missed lots of strikes but landed about a dozen cutthroats, several of them very big fish. A depressing moment, though, because I foul-hooked one in the eye. Jesus, I'm a killer.

But the evening couldn't be ruined. First came the caddis hatch. Then some mayflies. Then smaller mayflies. I fished and fished as mayflies swarmed over the water.

The sunset was particularly striking. There seems to be a lot of smoke and haze from the forest fires. The smell of charred forest is growing stronger. It feels a little eerie.

July 19

A perplexing day on the Henry's Fork. Got defeated on the most beautiful ranch meadow in the world. I couldn't induce a single strike. I fished beetles, ants, and small PMDs. The water was covered with PMDs at one point, smaller than anything I had. I've never seen pale morning duns as small as this before. Those duns were barely visible drifting on the current.

Tricos swarmed over the water, too, and I couldn't do a thing. I even saw a few brown drakes fluttering around over by the riverbank. I cast to rises again and again, but couldn't match the hatch effectively, and couldn't divert those trout from whatever they were taking that day.

This is why I love the Henry's Fork. Idaho would be a good place to live. Maybe I should think about moving out here permanently, next to the Henry's Fork. But there's probably not too much work out here for a writer like myself. Maybe I could make my living as a fishing guide, and open up a fly shop. Ah, the romance of fly fishing. It was an old fantasy I had. But it's probably not a good idea to turn your hobby into your work. I've noticed that the only people who don't have tans in summer here are the people who own the five fly shops in West Yellowstone. They're so busy in the high season, they never have a chance to get on the water. And what if I became bored with it all; what if I came to hate fly fishing?

JULY 20

I took eight cutthroats out of the Yellowstone below Buffalo Ford. I took them all on comparaduns—must buy some more, I'm all out.

At midday a rumbling came out of the dense lodgepoles. I looked up from my fishing. The rumbling grew louder, and bison appeared out of the trees. They were about to ford the Yellowstone, an entire herd. Fishermen hastily cleared a path for them. Bison won't detour around anyone or anything. On and on they came, shoulder-deep in the river. Bulls, females, bellowing calves—I counted ninety-six bison making the crossing.

The fires are getting closer—I can smell them advancing. The fires are a real presence inside the park now. Everyone is talking about them.

JULY 21

Took the day off. No fishing.

I listened to some interesting radio reports about the forest fires. They're getting bigger. Fire crews have arrived from the Pacific Northwest. The park's policy had been to let fires inside the park boundary burn, and people are now criticizing the park service for failing to get a jump on the fires and contain them. But there are three fires burning out of control outside the park boundaries, too, and all efforts to put them out have failed, despite the fact that firefighters began battling them the moment they erupted. It's just too hot and dry out here to contain these fires, the burn index is too high, and all the vegetation is at the cured stage and ready to ignite.

July 22

Fished the Yellowstone below Buffalo Ford again. It was a very hot and windy day, and there were no hatches or rises. I left early and got back to West Yellowstone around 5:30 P.M.

I hear on the radio that the South Entrance to the park might have to be closed because of the fires.

July 23

I had a good day fishing dry flies on the lower Madison River outside the park. I struck four and landed three big rainbows on the stretch of river near Raynold's Pass. I probably would have done better if I'd switched from drys to big Stonefly Nymphs. It was hot and, to my tastes, a little overcrowded on this stretch. But who am I to complain—I've been fishing with the crowds at Buffalo Ford, haven't I?

There are really huge fires burning in Yellowstone Park now. They're thinking of evacuating Grant Village. Things are going to get real interesting.

July 24

The South Entrance of Yellowstone National Park is closed. Grant Village has been evacuated for the first time in the park's history.

I fished on the Henry's Fork today and watched the black anvil of smoke gathering over the Yellowstone Plateau. This is the worst fire season anyone remembers. The drought has turned the woods to tinder.

The drought even seems to be affecting the insect hatches on Railroad Ranch. It's more like late August than mid-July out here. A scant few PMDs came off the stream, but I managed to catch a couple of trout.

July 25

Drove up to the canyon of the Beartrap on the Madison River. It's the wrong time of year to fish the Beartrap, but there's no sense in going into the park. Yellowstone is really burning. No one has ever seen anything like it before. One fire is already within ten miles of Old Faithful.

July 26

The fires in Yellowstone Park are immense and out of control. Nothing can contain them. Seventeen hundred firefighters from even western states are fighting a dozen separate conflagrations. The sky over the park is as black as a storm over the ocean. Two fires are burning outside the park, too. The South Entrance remains closed. Twenty thousand vacationers are still in Yellowstone. This is the worst fire in the recorded history of Yellowstone Park.

But none of this will keep me from fishing. I fished the Gallatin near the Taylor's Fork. Earlier in the morning I'd tried to fish hoppers on the Gallatin inside the park's borders. The river is low but cool and swift and comes as a welcome relief.

July 27

Eighty thousand trees in Yellowstone Park have burned. People are pissing and moaning about how the park is being destroyed but this is pure rot. The alarmist news media isn't helping put things in perspective, either. Look at me—already I'm complaining about my ex-profession. News reporters are such idiots. Don't they understand that forest fires represent renewal and not destruction? It certainly hasn't taken me long to begin to hate newspapers.

I fished the lower Madison near the Morgan Ranch, and did only okay on hoppers and stoneflies. I looked up to see thunderclouds on the horizon and then realized I was looking at a forty-thousand-foot-high convection column rising out of Yellowstone. The fires were blotting out the sun.

July 28

Fished the Madison at Raynold's Pass. The trout were hitting Black Stonefly Nymphs. The biggest fish bent the rod deeply before the leader broke.

July 29

Took a day off from fishing.

Someone from a radical environmental organization has been quoted in a newspaper as saying that the Yellowstone fires were only tragic in the sense that they had not destroyed the tourist facilities at Fishing Bridge. My sentiments exactly.

July 30

Nailed a big rainbow at Slide Inn on the Madison. That was about all the action anybody saw on the river today. Sunny and very hot, as per usual. It has become evident to just about everyone that the Yellowstone fires will continue burning out of control until the first rains of autumn come.

July 31

A windy afternoon on the Yellowstone at Raynold's Pass. Rain clouds were seen forming in the evening. Is there to be any relief? Maybe I should think about leaving.

August 1

Winds still fanning the Yellowstone fires. It's a wild scene, getting worse all the time. The fire is closing in on Old Faithful. It's threatening to burn down the Old Faithful Inn, which *would* be a tragedy because the inn really is an architectural masterpiece with its rustic, high-timber beams, one of the most interesting buildings in the West.

I caught a seventeen-inch brown trout at Raynold's Pass. It suddenly occurs to me that I'm getting bored with trout fishing. Maybe it really is time to move on.

On a morning in early August, as the park fires were growing and spreading, I hiked down to the Railroad Ranch water with Skip Gibson, a guide I'd met in West Yellowstone. It was Skip's day off. The guys who fish on their days off really are fanatics. I hauled Skip's fly vest out of the back of my Honda; it must have weighed twenty or thirty pounds.

"Jesus, I doubt they carry packs this heavy in the infantry," I told him.

The trout on the Railroad Ranch water were rising to tricos and pale morning duns, but Skip and I didn't start catching anything until we switched to small black caddisflies. Skip caught six trout; I caught one.

Afterward I told Skip I was thinking about clearing out of West Yellowstone. "I'm bored with trout fishing," I said.

"Where will you go?" he asked.

"I've never been steelhead fishing before. I think I'd like to see some rivers flowing into the Pacific Ocean."

"You've *got* to go to the North Umpqua," said Skip, suddenly animated. "And the Kalama River in Washington, too. You'll definitely want to fish the Kalama. I was talking with one of the firejumpers in the Stagecoach bar the other night. This guy's from Oregon. He told me that the North Umpqua was fishing great the week before he left to come out here."

"What do I need?" I asked Skip.

"A big rod," he said. "And maybe bigger balls."

I left Yellowstone the next day, having a final close-up look at the black sky over the park. Gazing at the terrible pall of smoke hanging there, I couldn't help but wonder if I might be burning something behind me, too.

Seven

SOMETIMES YOU THINK ABOUT OREGON

I drove out of Montana and into the heat and vastness of Oregon's eastern desert. It was a hundred degrees at midday in the canyon of the Deschutes. At Bend the high desert met the Cascades and I turned west toward the cooling plateau of Diamond Lake. Here the forests of skinny lodgepole gave way to dense stands of Douglas fir.

I saw the Umpqua for the first time, spraying through its fir-lined canyon. The river reflected the colors of the forest and sky. It appeared to be a wild, demanding river of ledge rocks and pools that would require long casts, sure footing, and wading up to the armpits in spots.

The North Umpqua spilled over dark basalt ledges, its pools essentially long channels cut out of the volcanic bedrock. An immense and shadowy evergreen forest screened the river, contributing to its multiple tints. The mountains were heavily mantled in Douglas firs and massive sugar pines growing up the slopes and along the sheltering benches. Towering trees leaned out over the banks, adding cooling shade to the stream. It looked deep and a little dangerous, passing untamed under the conifers, spilling in frothing rapids, filling dark volcanic fissures, squeezing between high banks covered by thick forest. The local Indians had named this river *Umpqua*—"thunder water."

I pulled over to take a good look at the river. A fresh breeze carried the perfume of wild blackberries growing on the north bank. As I admired the glide of the river a hundred feet below me, a steelhead broke the tranquillity with a silver flash and plunge. Skip had told me about steelhead: strong as ocean fish, smart as river trout.

I drove to the Steamboat Inn, a landmark lodge on the river. Behind the inn half a dozen cabins formed a semicircle under the sugar pines. A hundred feet below, the river thundered a greeting, lacy foam pouring into a green punch bowl called the Glory Hole.

I stepped into the inn's foyer. A painting of the Umpqua hung on the wall depicting a bluish mist rising out of an uncorked wine bottle. The winy fog turned into river water and pines, and a steelhead swam in the current like a guiding spirit.

In the main dining hall a fieldstone fireplace occupied one corner, and an elaborate glass cabinet displayed a huge array of fly-fishing paraphernalia. An antique fly-tying chest stood as tall as a dresser bureau. But my gaze held on the room's centerpiece, a richly burnished wooden table, easily twenty feet long. It had been planed from a single, massive slab of sugar pine and salvaged from a legendary steelhead camp across the river. Portraits of notable Umpqua anglers looked down from the walls. One portrait was unmistakable: that of Zane Grey.

The dining room opened onto a grape arbor where anglers hung their fly rods. A deck led out to cabins under the pine shade, and beyond the railings were magnificent views of the thundering river.

I noticed a thick stack of posters propped against one of the dining tables, all photographs of the North Umpqua. An inscription on the back of a poster read: J. DANIEL CALLAGHAN, CABIN ONE STUDIO. A nice touch: The photographer had named his studio after Cabin One in the Steamboat Inn. One photograph showed the inn itself, its pathway strewn with autumn leaves, windows glowing warm and yellow in a September dusk.

I introduced myself to the inn's owner, Jim Van Loan, and explained that I was a steelhead virgin. Van Loan had been a book salesman who had decided to buy the lodge on his favorite river. He quickly ran me through the basics of steelhead fishing and gave me some pointers for the Umpqua. "You might as well start on the Camp Water," he said.

I had read that Jack Hemingway once called the Camp Water, that section of river just upstream of the Steamboat Inn, "the greatest stretch of summer steelhead water in the United States."

So I was looking forward to this the way a teenager might antici-pate prom night.

Upriver, at the spot where Steamboat Creek enters the flow, I crossed a steel trestle bridge that spans the Umpqua. Steamboat Creek is the main tributary; the river doubles in width below it. I stopped in the middle of the span, known as Mott Bridge, to look upstream into a pool called Surveyor. The run was nestled in late-afternoon shade, and the Douglas firs seemed to be the size of old-growth redwoods. The river flowed over black volcanic bedrock channels.

At a small tree-shaded parking lot high above the Bridge Pool on the south bank, a wooden kiosk had been set up to welcome anglers to steelhead Valhalla. A detailed river map, carved out of a huge block of wood and set under glass, depicted all twenty-six pools on the Camp Water, with their names etched underneath the drawing.

A pathway called the Mott Trail, which was part of the larger North Umpqua Trail, led downriver, through shady stands of Douglas fir, red cedar, sugar pine, and vine maple. The Mott Trail, like Mott Bridge, was named after Major Lawrence Mott, an officer in the U.S. Army Signal Corps. In 1929, the year of the Great Crash, Mott established a rough tent camp for steelhead fishermen at Steamboat on land leased from the U.S. Forest Ser-vice. A photograph of the major hung in the Steamboat Inn. It was taken in 1930, the year before his death from cancer, and it showed the major standing with a calm military bearing, holding a thin bamboo fly rod in one hand and an immense king salmon in the other. He had snatched the fish from the Kitchen Pool.

An angler's path led through poison oak down to a shady pool known as the Sawtooth, named after a submerged reef. Another scramble path came out on a sweeping cobblestone bar overlooking a green channel known as the Lower Boat Pool. A third footpath ended at the Kitchen Pool, and this was the one I chose.

With much difficulty I waded out on the Kitchen's rocky ledges. It took me some time to figure out the route through a labyrinth of submerged ledge rock. I was unsure of my footing and stumbled frequently. The runnels on the river bottom were etched with many fine scratches made by the stream cleats worn by generations of anglers. I had taken the precaution of attaching carbide-studded soles to my wading boots. The sunken ledge rock was still dangerously slick. I had read somewhere that Vic O'Bern, a legendary Umpqua guide of the 1930s who kept a fishing camp downriver near the Salmon Racks, had drowned while wading the river.

Eventually I made it out onto the submerged ledge overlooking the deeper channels of the Kitchen Pool, which was filled with underwater ledges and sunken boulders. I stared into the channels and soon began seeing gray forms near the bottom. That shade of gray was not natural to the rubble of the streambed. These were steelhead, distinguished by their ghostly paleness.

A steelhead leapt into the air and landed with a smack not twenty feet from me. I almost fell into the river. I had never seen a rainbow trout the size of a mature salmon. My hands were shaking with excitement. I was outfitted with a nine-foot rod and a heavy line, and I began casting across and slightly downstream, as Jim Van Loan had advised. The idea was to let the fly swing through the water on an arc. I enjoyed the feeling of the coated line sliding back and forth through my rod guides and unrolling in the air. The sun on my face felt good as I watched my large streamer fly swimming through clean water.

I worked my way slowly down the Kitchen Pool, casting out as far as I could, letting the fly swing through the water about one or two inches under the surface, and then gingerly taking a few more steps downstream. By this means I managed to cover both the Upper and the Lower Kitchen, and soon I found myself standing on a rock overlooking a turbulent pool called the Fighting Hole. After casting over this several times without success, I fished my way down the three Mott Pools.

By now the afternoon shadows on the North Bank were stretching out over all the Camp Water pools. This cut down the glare, and the steelhead were easier to see. Still, nothing I did could induce a steelhead to rise to inspect my fly. Back up in the Kitchen Pool, I watched an angler playing a fish, his rod pulsing over a frantic boil in the water. The steelhead thrashed to the surface, spray flying everywhere. God, how I wanted one of those fish.

The river glided into evening's dimness. The dancing rapids below the Mott Pools appeared phosphorescent. Steelhead were all around. A few had leapt in front of me. I had watched half a dozen of them struggling on the ends of fly lines. But I hadn't gotten so much as a single bump.

I drove downriver to Susan Creek Campground and pitched my tent under its trees. Inside my sleeping bag the North Umpqua still flowed against me and inside me as I fell asleep.

The next morning I set out on the Mott Trail through the trees and ferns in the early light and shadows. At the Kitchen Pool I watched a steelhead jump and flash against a background of dark green conifers.

The fish were holed up in the kind of water favored by trout—in slots between submerged ledges, around boulders where the current eased, and in the rubble of the tailouts. The steelhead faced upstream, like river trout. When they became interested in something floating their way, they would tilt upward very slightly and move their fins a little faster. When they took notice of an angler, they didn't flee; instead they dropped slowly toward the bottom or sidled off just a bit to one side.

But steelhead exploded the moment a hook touched them. I watched a fish in the Station Pool jump five or six times immediately after a fly angler stuck it. The fish tried to race downstream into the rapids of the Upper Boat Pool before the struggling angler managed to check the flight. Had it reached white water, that steelhead would have been more than capable of spooling the angler's reel.

The Station Pool was the best fishing on the Camp Water. It lies directly downstream of the river's confluence with Steamboat Creek. Steamboat is the Umpqua's main spawning tributary, and steelhead tend to rest below the creek's mouth. They remain in these holes most of the summer, until the rains of late October raise the level of the river, signaling the fish to continue upstream on their spawning run. One angler after another took steelhead out of the Station Pool, but I had no success there. I found it a difficult spot to reach and had trouble working my way out through the riffles into the channel. Other anglers seemed to have little problem fording it.

I fished Hayden's Run and Sawtooth and the three Mott Pools. The Lower Kitchen kept drawing me back, with its underwater rock ledges and what appeared to be prime steelhead holding water. But the pool I fell in love with above all others was the Surveyor, directly above the old Mott Bridge. This was the first pool in the Camp Water to slip into shade, and I sought it out because steelhead fishing is always said to be best with the sun off the water.

I got three electrifying taps on my fly at the Surveyor Pool. The first turned out to be a tiny steelhead smolt. The other two were juvenile trout of five or six inches. What a disappointment.

I met Frank Moore on the Upper Kitchen Pool. It was evening, and I was watching an elderly gentleman moving along the submerged ledges with a degree of nimbleness wholly inappropriate to his age. He positioned himself to fish around a large, protruding boulder known as the Kitchen Rock. The white-haired angler waded out almost up to his armpits and effortlessly laid out a great amount of line. His casts were very straight, and he wasted no energy. He made a few quick passes behind Kitchen Rock and then climbed out.

Moore introduced himself. What stood out was his strong, kind face. I was not prepared for the comfortable feeling that I experienced in the man's presence. Even I knew who Frank Moore was. A former proprietor of the Steamboat Inn, Moore is widely regarded as one of the finest steelhead fisherman in Oregon, and a link between the river's glorious angling past and its present.

I told Moore I was a steelhead greenhorn. He examined my fly and said, "They like flies a little larger on this river." He showed me what he was using: something big and purple. He seemed genuinely interested in my catching my first steelhead.

A fish shattered the surface of the Lower Kitchen Pool, leaving a massive wake, rings widening and slowly disappearing on the water.

"That steelhead was *huge*," I whispered.

"That was probably a salmon," said Moore. "Oh sure, we get salmon coming up with the steelhead in summer." He explained that fly fishermen usually didn't bother with the bottom-hugging salmon, preferring the topwater sport that steelhead offered. Moore told me that Umpqua steelhead could be taken on dry flies in the lower stream flows of summer.

This river has seen a lot of history, and Frank Moore was a huge part of it. He had taken over proprietorship of the Steamboat Inn from Clarence Gordon, himself a legendary steelhead fisherman and guide on the North Umpqua during the 1930s. It was Clarence Gordon who had acquired the old Mott camp on the south bank at Steamboat. Shortly before his death from leukemia in 1931, Major Mott had arranged to have his tent camp pass to his chief guide and cook, Zeke Allen. In 1934 Gordon, a sportsman from southern California, won approval from the forest service to take over Allen's camp concession. Gordon had fallen in love with the Umpqua while passing through Oregon on his way to fish up in Canada. Gordon raised his kitchen tent on land overlooking what came to be known as the Kitchen Pool. With the encouragement of forest service officials he built a permanent lodge with cabins, a fieldstone fireplace, and a dining hall. He christened his resort the North Umpqua Lodge, and many of his sportsman friends from southern California came up to visit. Soon word began to spread about the extraordinary steelhead fishing found on the North Umpqua. Gordon hosted

Ray Bergman, a fishing writer for *Outdoor Life,* who further publicized the river.

In Gordon's day the canyon was a truly wild and fairly remote place. The only access was by a dirt road high above the river. The pools under the conifers were as well defined as the holes on a golf course, and soon they were christened by Gordon, his guides, and local fishermen. Gordon became known as a fearless wader as well as an innovative fly tier. He created the eponymous Black Gordon, then the most popular fly on the river.

But things change, and rivers don't remain the same. In time the canyon began to lose its isolation, and with it a small measure of its primal beauty. By the 1950s a two-lane asphalt road was under construction along the river's grade, and a dam was being built upstream at Soda Springs. When the forest service decided to build a headquarters on the south bank at Steamboat on the very land occupied by the North Umpqua Lodge, Gordon lost his lease. He salvaged what he could from his lodge, including that magnificent dining table hewn from a single slab of sugar pine, and opened a store on the north bank near Steamboat Creek, on a small patch of land he leased from the forest service. Later he shifted his operation a quarter mile downstream to the site of what became the Steamboat Inn. There were more construction workers on the river than fishermen. Debris from the highway and dam construction put the river out of shape; some seasons it wasn't fishable at all. Anglers went looking elsewhere for their sport.

By 1957, however, road and dam construction was complete and the North Umpqua had returned to a nearly pristine state—but of course the canyon was accessible to anyone with a car. It was then that Clarence Gordon decided to pull up stakes and return to California. He was getting on in years, and the Umpqua was no longer the unspoiled river he had known and loved. That's when Frank Moore came into the picture. Moore was one of Gordon's steelhead guides, and such a good angler that it was rumored that Gordon had hired him mainly to keep him from competing with Gordon's guests on the river. When Frank Moore heard Gordon was going to put the Steamboat Inn up for sale, he talked Colonel Jim Hayden, one of Gordon's sports from southern California, into floating him a loan. Moore renovated the restaurant and store and built guest cabins on a shelf of sugar pines just below the main building. He was to run Steamboat Inn for the next twenty years, as well as serving on the Oregon Fish and Game Commission, where he gained a reputation as a staunch conservationist.

In the meantime, with the river coming back into shape, regular guests of Gordon's old lodge were returning to the Umpqua and staying at the Steamboat Inn. As the river's reputation continued to grow, the Umpqua began once again to attract its share of world-class fishermen. After all, Zane Grey had fished the North Umpqua. So, too, had fishing writers Ray Bergman, Claude Kreider, and Clark Van Fleet back in the 1930s and '40s. Roderick

Haig-Brown paid a visit. Jack Hemingway, the eldest son of novelist Ernest Hemingway, became a frequent guest at Moore's lodge, and he introduced his friend, the fishing writer Ernest Schwiebert, to the river. Hemingway was fishing the river from the Steamboat Inn in the summer of 1961 when he received an emergency telephone call informing him that his father had shot himself in Sun Valley. Moore, a licensed pilot, flew Jack Hemingway and his wife, Puck, to Idaho for the funeral.

"Try and keep your fly moving at the speed of the current," Frank Moore advised me. "You don't want it to swing around too fast. Steelhead don't much care for it when a fly moves too fast. Do you know how to mend line?" Moore demonstrated with an upstream flip of his fly line.

"Did you know Zane Grey?" I asked.

Moore smiled and shook his head. How old did this kid think he was, anyway? Moore told me he sold the Steamboat Inn to its present owners, Jim and Sharon Van Loan, in 1975; he and his wife, Jeanne, lived in a log home he had built under the Douglas firs high above the river at Fairview, affording them a spectacular view. Moore said he was planning a September trip to the Clearwater River in Idaho, where the steelhead were much larger than the fish here. But the North Umpqua was the river he loved and cherished above all others. He wished me success and clambered off to fish another pool, moving over the Kitchen's flooded ledges with grace and confidence. The underwater route must have been imprinted on his brain. It was twilight, and the silvery rapids upstream were turning evanescent.

By no means did I restrict myself to fishing the Camp Water. There were noteworthy pools downstream, too, and all held steelhead, depending on water levels and seasonal conditions. The next morning I worked the Ledges, a pool named by Zane Grey. And on subsequent days I fished the Upper and Lower Archie as well as the Log Pool, Discovery, Split Rock, and Burnham. None surrendered any fish to me. At midafternoon I tried my hand at the Wright Creek Pool and Famous Pool, the first pool upstream of the fly-fishing boundary. These two pools had reputations for producing fish at midday, with the sun shining on the water, but I had no success there.

Because it was well into summer, steelhead also held upstream of the Camp Water, in pools with names like the Upper and Lower Redman, Panther Leap, Charcoal Point, and Eagle Rock. In fact, steelhead were showing up just about everywhere in the thirty-one miles of river canyon that had been set aside exclusively for fly angling.

The creation of the fly-only section occurred back in 1951, when Clarence Gordon, backed by the membership of the Roseburg Rod and Gun Club, convinced the Oregon Fish and Game Commission that angling restrictions were needed to protect declining steelhead and salmon stocks on the North

Umpqua. So the commission decided to set aside the canyon from Rock Creek upstream to the dam at Soda Springs for fly anglers—one of the first rivers in the country to be classified as fly fishing only. This was defined as angling with traditional fly-rod methods or with spinning gear equipped with a fly and a floating plastic bubble. Because it was felt that North Umpqua steelhead deserved the sanctuary of deeper water, lead and other weight attachments to a line were outlawed. For the Roseburg Rod and Gun Club, whose members were not all fly anglers, the victory became a case of the adage "Be careful what you wish for, for it might come true." Over the ensuing years, the club membership tried unsuccessfully to repeal the fly-only regulation to allow for bait and spin fishing. But the rule has remained in effect up to the present time, and it appears unlikely that it will ever change.

I hooked and lost my first steelhead at the Divide Pool above the Williams Creek riffle. The Divide is one of the first steelhead runs downstream of the Camp Water pools. The riffle, broad and wadable for the most part and pouring downstream for several hundred yards, appeared eminently fishable. My line was passing through the water in its usual arc when suddenly the rod jolted in my hand. I raised it and felt a living, kicking weight on the end of the line. But seemingly before it registered that I truly had hooked a steelhead, my line went slack. The fish had come free. I lifted my head and howled at the trees. But it proved to me that steelhead would come to my casts.

Williams Creek, not far from this spot, had been the site of Zane Grey's last fishing camp on the river. Of all the anglers who have fished the North Umpqua, Zane Grey is by far the most famous.

The novelist arrived on the river in the summer of 1932, his entourage in tow. With him were his sons, Romer and Loren, the author's friends, hired hands, fishing guides, secretaries, a still photographer and movie cameraman, and a Japanese field cook, George Takahashi, a cheerful, diminutive fellow who often appeared as a comic foil speaking pidgin English in Zane Grey's fishing stories. Merle Hargis, a mule skinner employed by the National Forest Service, packed in Grey's considerable baggage—three trips' worth. America's richest author paid Hargis exactly two bucks.

Zane Grey's Western genre novels had made him what today would be the equivalent of a multimillionaire. His royalties provided him the fortune he needed to mount fishing campaigns of imperial size. After the success of *Riders of the Purple Sage* in 1912, Grey, a onetime dentist, who had become America's best-selling author, was free to fish anywhere on the globe. Writing competed with fishing as Zane Grey's ruling passion. His expeditions took him to Oak Creek Canyon in Arizona, Newfoundland, New Zealand, and the blue waters of the Pacific. In 1922 Grey discovered steelhead fishing on Oregon's Rogue River. He became a great publicist for the river, and the Rogue featured in many of his fishing stories. But the river he came to love above all others was the North Umpqua.

Dissatisfied with the accommodations offered by Zeke Allen, Grey established more elaborate encampments along the river, first at the confluence of Steamboat and Canton creeks; then on the north bank directly across from Zeke Allen's camp; at Maple Ridge Point, the present site of the Steamboat Inn; and finally downriver at Williams Creek, where he raised his tent camp, fishing in the early morning and cranking out books at midday.

Grey might have been the best-known angler ever to fish the river, but he was easily the most disliked. In a preface to the only story he ever published about the North Umpqua, Grey said he seriously doubted that the people of Oregon were suited to the task of protecting it. "It is difficult to talk to people who are not particularly interested in the value of a river," he wrote condescendingly. The editors at *Sports Afield* balked at publishing this preface, and it did not see the light of print until well after Grey's death, when it appeared in an anthology of his fishing stories.

Grey's paternalism did not win him many friends on the Umpqua. Although more than half a century has passed since Grey last fished the river, there are still a few survivors around who remember him vividly, if not fondly. Merle Hargis, in his eighties and still living beside the river, has told interviewers that Grey couldn't abide other people fishing his favorite pools, especially bait fishermen, whom he regarded as not fully developed human beings. Hargis recalled that George Takahashi, Grey's cook, once chased his younger brother away from the camp. Dave Asam, the son of Fred Asam, who was the district ranger on the river in those days, recalled that Grey once tried to bribe Dave and his sister Nina away from swimming in one of Grey's pools. Nina told the millionaire off, saying he didn't have enough money to buy the kids off their own river. Grey also made a practice of hiring flunkies to guard prime steelhead pools until the author got first crack at them. These underlings would position themselves in the pools at first light and stand there pretending to fish until the author showed up to explore them at his leisure. Naturally, this rubbed other anglers the wrong way.

Just exactly how unpopular Zane Grey was is evidenced in the names locals gave their river pools. Two pools on the North Umpqua were named after Fred Burnham, Grey's friend and an expert steelhead angler who first taught the author how to fly fish for steelhead on the Rogue. And not one but two Camp Water pools honor Grey's cook Takahashi, who won the hearts of the locals. But not a single pool on the North Umpqua was ever christened with the name of its most famous angling celebrity.

There was an ugly, competitive streak in Grey. It showed most dramatically in his pursuit of billfish records. Grey once challenged Ernest Hemingway to a deep-sea-fishing contest, but Papa didn't pick up the gauntlet. During one ill-fated bluewater foray off New Zealand, Grey failed to report Fred Burnham's catch, a record marlin, possibly because it might have topped one of his own world records. The two men never spoke after that.

Grey was dozing in camp at Williams Creek on an oppressively hot morning in July 1937, a day when temperatures in the canyon were topping a hundred degrees. His son Romer returned from fishing to find his father slumped unconscious in a chair. At first it was suspected that Grey had suffered heatstroke. But it was a real stroke, a cerebral hemorrhage, and it left the author temporarily paralyzed. Grey spent the next two years at home in Altadena, in southern California, recuperating, dictating books, recounting fishing adventures, and planning new ones. But he never fully recovered. Early one morning in 1939 Grey collapsed at home, dead of a massive rupture of the right ventricle.

Dr. Loren Grey, Zane Grey's surviving son, a psychologist by profession, has said in print that his father was a driven and unhappy man. There was a tragic flaw in him. But there was something magnificent, too, in his obsessions. When he was fifteen years old Grey wrote his first short story. It was about two buddies and their secret cave. Zane Grey's father discovered the manuscript, tore it to pieces in front of the shocked teenager, and then thrashed his son, ordering young Zane never again to waste his time on anything as frivolous as writing. Zane Grey went on to write and publish nine million words. At the end of his life, his complete oeuvre amounted to eighty published books and some

250 magazine articles on hunting, fishing, the outdoors, and conservation. *Riders of the Purple Sage* sold more than a million copies in hardback alone; in all, 130 million copies of his books sold worldwide in two dozen languages. Not a bad epitaph for the boy who was forbidden to write.

You can lose yourself in fly fishing. That's to say you can lose your *self*. This steelhead fishing was beginning to turn me into something of a manic depressive. Anglers were catching steelhead upstream and downstream of me, and I had yet to land my first. Well, Zane Grey had trouble catching his first Rogue River steelhead, too; maybe I had to pay my dues on the Umpqua. I fished in something of a dream state. A pattern of repetition imprinted itself on my brain from the endless casts I made across and downstream.

I received no end of consolation. Everyone told me the Umpqua was *hard*. A graduate school. A finishing school. The hardest steelhead to catch in the world. For hours the steelhead would lie like sunken logs in the mumbling river. And then they would begin to roll or jump for no discernible reason. Why did they jump? Why did they take flies at all? Why did they ignore mine? But I was beginning to understand the river a little better. And I was convinced that anyone who could handle a fly rod reasonably well should be able to catch a steelhead.

Learning the river was the most enjoyable part. One morning I watched leaping steelhead at Deadline Falls. Deadline is the major waterfall in the canyon; rafters and kayakers have to get out and portage there. Deadline is a classic example of a block falls, where powerful plunging waters descend in a wide stream. Umpqua steelhead and salmon on their way to spawn in the tributary waters of the Cascade Mountains have to make the ascent of Deadline.

Restless steelhead milled and cruised at the foot of the falls. They stirred constantly in preparation for the big leap. They were preoccupied with the problem of ascension, gathering their strength for the assault. I would watch them jumping, singly and in pairs, producing dramatic, apparently reckless leaps. But these were in fact carefully calculated attempts.

Steelhead do not make long runs at the falls. Rather, like salmon, they come up from under the base. At the very foot of the plunging waterfall they propel themselves upward in short, lunging thrusts. The splashing water rebounding upward from the plunge is used to the fullest advantage. I watched them start at the bottom and come out of the foam, shooting far up the cataract. Swimming furiously, they entered the slanting torrent and seemed to hold there for a minisecond. They used all their pent-up power to climb the vertical current of the falls. They were actually swimming in water that was falling through air. Their great vitality was measured against the hazardous trip and the gauntlet of dangers they faced.

∽ ∽ ∽ ∽ ∽ ∽

One of the most dramatic pools on the river is the Riprap. A spectacular vertical rock rises out of the timber on the south bank. Emerald mosses and yellowish lichens cover its face, and a boulder-strewn channel lies beneath it, with a steep rapid just downstream. The river narrows here, filling a volcanic fissure. I was practicing a technique called a Crossfield hitch. It involves twitching the rod horizontally to induce a take as the fly swings through the water on its arc. I saw a good fish flash under my fly. But I struck too soon. The steelhead receded to the bottom and didn't come up again.

At the Surveyor Pool, in the Camp Water, another angler gave me a crash course in tying and fishing a riffling hitch. A riffling hitch causes a damp fly to fish on the surface like a skating dry. It involves securing a knot to one side of the hook eye, which forces the fly to rise up and skim along in the surface film. In my trout fishing I had discovered that trout tended to be terrified of a dragging fly, but for some reason a wake seemed to trigger a strike response in steelhead. I was assured that the take would be very dramatic on a riffling hitch. I was never to know how dramatic, however, because I could never get an adult steelhead to take it. Naturally, steelhead smolts ate it like candy.

By now I was in a serious funk: Seven days on the river and all I had to show was a series of flashes, nicks, and bumps, plus one fish hooked and lost in an instant. I was beginning to fear I was setting some kind of record for ineptitude on the North Umpqua.

∾ ∾ ∾ ∾ ∾ ∾

The next morning, in the shadows of the Surveyor Pool, where I regularly began my daily fishing, I decided to tie on a dry fly. All the anglers I met on the river had told me how hard it was to take a North Umpqua steelhead on a dry fly. To make matters worse, I cast directly upstream and let the fly float back to me on a dead drift. This was said to be the hardest way of all. To my astonishment, a steelhead rose immediately and swallowed the fly. I felt the fish's weight and raised the rod. Pop! The leader, which tested at a full ten pounds, broke. I let loose a torrent of Anglo-Saxon epithetical fricatives.

I tried telling myself that if this were easy, it would soon lose much of its appeal. I rested the pool while tying on another fly. The Surveyor was beautiful, colored by reflected trees and black volcanic basalt. Buoying water drawn upward from the pool's center gained speed as it glided toward the tailout. My eyes tried to adjust to the underwater vagaries. The distortions blurred and clarified, and somehow, through the refraction of light, I detected the presence of transparent shapes blending into the gravel and rocks of the river.

At first the shapes remained indistinct. But gradually these gray shadows emerged through the wavering lens to become a steelhead. A bit of darkness outlined a dorsal. That small patch of white might be an opening mouth.

I quartered my cast and watched the floating line being carried downstream by the water. My large caddisfly began to skate across the surface, creating a bold V-shaped wake.

The first indication I had was a barely perceptible bulge just under the fly. Did I imagine that? A second cast confirmed my first impression—a shape clearly rose off the bottom, only to sink back again.

While a steelhead's strike might be anticipated, it is never fully expected. Although it had been the major focus of my thoughts for the past week, when the moment finally arrived it came as a complete shock to me. On the next cast, after what felt like thousands of traveled arcs over a series of dreamlike days, a steel-gray shadow emerged from the bottom and, when it reached just the right depth and angle of light penetration, turned into a rainbow spectrum. My fly disappeared in a swirl. The rod bent, and the pool erupted in a shower of spray.

The steelhead jumped and flashed before the backdrop of trees. It jumped two more times in what seemed like a frozen moment. It was one of those instants when you seem to step back from your life. A gigantic, kicking boil emerged where once there had been only current. The rod pulsed as the river's living power seemed to run up my arm. The steelhead gleamed as it thrashed at the surface.

The fish sounded and shook its head. It felt remarkably heavy—I had never felt a trout like it. The steelhead made a run downstream and then up, and I had just enough presence of mind to check its flight by palming the reel. The steelhead leapt again and got below me. There was a tremendous bend in the rod, and it quivered and pulsed and dipped downward. I felt certain that all the power of this Pacific wanderer was mustered to break me off. The steelhead thumped in the current and the rod vibrated dangerously close to breaking.

My steelhead made a boiling rush to the head of the pool. And then it dropped slowly downcurrent, tugging and jerking all the while. I applied all my tackle would stand. The fish seemed to be out of leaps now. Surely it was tiring, tugging and pulling on the line, becoming almost deadweight. I brought the fish toward me headfirst, and when the great trout saw me, it exploded again into fits of fury and panic.

I needed ten or fifteen minutes to land that fish, my first steelhead. It was a hen, eight pounds of silver and rose transparency. The fish was bullet shaped with a silver sheen. There was a faint wash of color in the transition zones between her dark metallic back and her silver sides, a light lavender cast that seemed to change depending on the angle of my head and how I held her. This shining lavender wash blended and deepened into rose luminescence along her lateral lines. And this hue seemed to fade in and out and run onto her pale belly as a light pink wash. All of these hues blended together under that incredible sheen of silver. There was enough subtle shifting and mirror shimmering to light a room.

Naturally, a gift this generous had to be returned undamaged to the North Umpqua. I released my steelhead back into the water and watched her swim off under her own power. My legs could still feel the movement of the river, and I hated to leave it.

Fly fishing holds moments when the shapeliness of life is almost literary. I was no longer a mere spectator, but a participant. This was the river of Zane Grey and Clarence Gordon and Frank Moore, and now, I suppose, it was my river, too. I was overjoyed to be a small part of it.

Eight

HOLY WATER

The Kalama River wends its way through the gorges and timbered hills of southwestern Washington State. Its headwaters drain the southern slope of Mount St. Helens, the youngest volcano in the Cascade Range. I had good views of Mount St. Helens in the distance, its elegant snow cone sweeping downward toward a bristling pine forest. You could sell Rainier Beer and Airstream trailers with scenery like this. I was punchy from driving and frankly starting to weary of the freshness in nature. On the road too long, I was beginning to feel like Charles Kuralt's evil twin.

But I'd had a taste of steelhead fishing and I wanted more. An angler on the Umpqua told me about Pigeon Springs on a stretch of the Kalama River called the Holy Water. He said the Kalama was much like a smaller version of the Umpqua.

The southern-flowing Kalama had been spared the horrible destruction that occurred when the north face of Mount St. Helens blew its nose on a Sunday morning in May 1980. An ash cloud rose ninety thousand feet, darkening the orchard country of eastern Washington. The surface of the north face avalanched downward at two hundred miles an hour, burying the Toutle River and wiping out its steelhead run. Fifty-nine people were killed, including crusty old Harry Truman, a darling of newspaper and television reporters, who, in the best old-coot tradition, had refused repeated warnings by government officials to clear out of his cabin before the mountain blew.

I had a little trepidation about fishing the Kalama River, but not because of any leftover destruction; the Kalama, being on the south side of the volcano, had been spared. I was more worried about the logging. The Weyerhaeuser Company had been actively logging the Pacific Northwest. The company's operations had been so rapacious that some out-of-state reporters covering the volcanic eruption had difficulty distinguishing ground zero from the clear-cuts.

I wanted to see if the Kalama would meet my exacting standard for a wilderness experience, which is a river without a Coke machine on its banks.

The Kalama is not a huge stream, as rivers go. The lower drifts pass through pastoral dairy land and farm country before emptying into the broad Columbia near the town of Kalama. A two-lane road follows the river up into its timbered gorge.

The riverbanks were lush, framed by western hemlock and deep green mosses, lichens, and maidenhair ferns. A tributary spring bubbled up under a Douglas fir, looking clear enough to drink from. The scent of ripening blackberries wafted into the warm August sunshine. The steep banks were shady and cool, with vine maples, alders, and pointed evergreens growing in profusion.

I had expected the music of band saws. Instead I heard a faint chamber music rising up from under the trees, the strings and oboes of the Kalama River. The Kalama flowed swiftly in its shaded canyon. It was impossible to look down at the tumbling river and not believe a steelhead might seize your fly.

I found Prichard's Western Anglers, a bait and tackle shop, nestled under the Douglas firs near the river. I picked up a license and got the lowdown on fishing conditions.

Kalama River Road followed the stream up the timbered corridor. Morning sunshine passed through evergreens. The light on the river penetrated down into what appeared superficially as shallow pools, illuminating a jumble of stones, boulders, and underwater shelves. The summer river looked low and very clear.

There were plenty of parking turnouts under the trees. From my vantage point on the high bank, the river looked like prime steelhead water, with green pools, bouldered tailouts, and swift runs that held good-looking pocket water. It all seemed ideal for fly fishing.

I wanted to see the Holy Water, so I followed the road up the canyon. The Holy Water is a three-mile stretch in the narrow gorge between Summer Creek Bridge and Gobar Creek Bridge. It's one of the most famous stretches of steelhead water in Washington, perhaps in the United States. The Holy Water is restricted to fly fishing. It was named by Mike Kennedy, a steelhead fly-fishing pioneer of the 1930s. I wanted to see the Honey Hole, Kennedy's favorite pool. And the Washboard, an underwater ledge near Pigeon Springs, named after the bandtail pigeons that perch in the Douglas firs. From the road I saw rocky waterfalls, deep pools, and fast, broken water.

The Holy Water looked little different from the river downstream. The hills above me were scabbed over in places. A logging truck almost blew me off the road. The canyon was thick with overgrowth and shade. I spotted a brilliant western tanager flashing yellow and orange in the sunshine.

In a clearing in the forest I spotted an old fern picker's cabin. It was a remnant of bygone days. Ragged strips of tar hung down like streamers from the roof. The cedar shakes had been bleached and weathered by years of sun and rain. The derelict cabin had been used by fern pickers who visited the canyon to gather the feathery fronds once in demand by floral shops in Portland and Vancouver.

I pulled into one of the turnouts and looked for a likely place to begin my fishing. Below me a river pool showed clear in the sunlight. A well-worn footpath led down the steep bank to the river. I scrambled down for a closer look. I could see a steelhead on the bottom of the pool, swaying slightly from side to side, its jaws opening and closing. It seemed like a gray ghost suspended in a kind of metaphysical ether.

The summer steelhead in the Kalama River averaged seven to ten pounds, like the fish in the North Umpqua River. A few might go larger. They were summer-run fish. They had been in the river for some time now, but they would still be bright and full of energy.

Summer steelhead start arriving in the Kalama River sometime around May. The peak of the run usually occurs in July, but fresh steelhead keep arriving all summer and fall. The fishing is splendid until the end of October. Salmon and searun cutthroat trout follow the steelhead into the river as the first bright tints of autumn begin appearing along the banks.

The river seemed tuned to a perfect pitch. I swear I heard all thirteen cellos of the Philadelphia Orchestra down there. I felt swallowed up in jumbled stands of Douglas fir, red cedar, vine maple, and, nearer the water, dense thickets of alder. The river bottom was a crisscross of brown lava formations that cast shadows shielding the steelhead from prying eyes. The water was much deeper than it had looked from above: The extreme clarity was deceiving. I found a place to wade in, at the head of a dark run of water fanning out into yards of streaming river that sparkled and danced in the light.

The summer river was beautiful. In many ways it reminded me of the North Umpqua, only smaller. The studs I was wearing on my wading boots bit through the green algae on the rocks, giving me a surefooted grip. They also aided me in negotiating the steep banks.

I tied on a dry fly and whispered a cast over the flowing water. I had been told a summer steelhead might move as much as twenty feet to seize a teasing fly.

I fished upstream first, dead drift. Then downstream, skating the fly so as to create a wake on the surface. After I covered the pool in this fashion, I switched to a streamer and began to fish it an inch or two under the surface. The streamer fly was black and green. Green and black were the colors of the shadowy river, and I felt that this fly might give me a kind of sympathetic magic.

I cast the fly with the long rod and gently mended to adjust for the crosscurrents. As the fly began to belly out, I rolled a loose loop of line upstream, as delicately as possible so as not to jerk the fly. The fly played slowly in the fluctuating current and the line eased its way across the pool.

Once I thought I saw the water bulge around the fly, but I couldn't be sure if a steelhead had risen to inspect it. I had forgotten to bring my polarized sunglasses into the canyon and I had trouble peering into the glare. The narrow, timbered canyon provided the river with its share of shade, however, and I tried to take advantage of it.

I inched my way through tailing shallows, squinting into the water for a glimpse of a steelhead. A steelhead rose out of the sunlit riffles and seized my fly in its jaws. I pulled back on the tugging weight and the fly came loose. Well, the steelhead were interested.

I fished over a jumble of rocks without coming upon another steelhead. I continued to fish on through the flowing fan of a tail-out, using a teasing retrieve to extend the swing. As I fished the fly through its swing I realized I had been picking up line too soon for my recast. The next time I let the fly hang twitching in the current directly below me. Three, four, five seconds passed. I looked over at a small brook spilling into the pool on the opposite bank. The fresh creek mouth frothed into the river. Suddenly there was a tug on my hovering fly and I pulled up on a steelhead.

It jumped several feet out of the water and fell back on its broad tail with a healthy splash. The water boiled around it, and the fish broke the surface again, cartwheeling.

The ratchet on my reel buzzed as the steelhead pulled line, wrenching wildly downstream. It threw spray, threatening to take its fight into the broken rapids below the pool. I strained and the rod bent under the power of the fish.

The steelhead plowed across the stream. It thrashed once again to the surface and then swam into the sanctuary of deeper water. I could feel six or seven pounds of steelhead all the way down into my rod grip. I couldn't help but think that I was trying to contain a powerhouse of river life.

The steelhead was sullenly shaking its head, burrowing downward. It swam with great deliberation over the rocky, sunshine-mottled bottom and bored into dark shadows. The fish shook its head a few more times, and there began a stalemate in the heaviest part of the current. And then abruptly and without warning, the fly simply came loose.

The sparkling green river continued to flow as if nothing out of the ordinary had happened. I could smell wild blackberries ripening on the steep bank behind me. Despite the loss of the steelhead, I felt both elated and soothed by the sound and sensation of the rushing water. It was beautiful to see and feel and hear the river.

I worked my way downstream to another rock-strewn pool. Again at the end of each swing, I dangled the fly in the churning water before beginning a retrieve. I gave the fly a good soak, bouncing it in the current. Again I felt another tug and was on to a steelhead. Had I cracked the code?

The fish struggled, churning water as it rose. It plowed across the stream, thrashing to the surface, flinging spray, swimming hard around the pool. I followed it, rod raised high, gaining line back on the reel. I could feel the fish's head shaking. I pumped and recovered more line and soon felt the steelhead's resolve weakening. Soon I was easing six pounds of bright steelhead onto the bank.

Surely the fish had heart. I was holding the wild life of the river in my hands. Water dripped off its silver-and-rose flanks. Feeling the fish trying to breathe, I cradled it in my arms and brought it back into the flowing water. Its head faced upstream; it reflected sunlight off its streaming back. I rocked the steelhead back and forth to allow water to move through its gills. After a minute of this, I stood up and watched it kick away under its own power, disappearing into the black-and-green river. The warmth of the sun felt good on my wet arms.

The summer canyon provided a series of alternating sights and auditory sensations. Dark and bright pools mirrored the greenery of vine maple, dogwood, and alder. The white noise of riffles, the gurgle of water around protruding stones, the whine of a cloud of gnats—these sounds were all absorbed into the thick tangle of trees, roots, and ferns.

Time passed on the river. Sunshine illuminated a cloud of mayflies above the water. The afternoon sun reached a certain angle and then sank below the treetops. I thought my chances might improve with the sun off the water. Every now and again a steelhead leapt into the air only to disappear back into the rushing river.

A lid of shadow fell across the gray rocks and bubbling water. Somewhere back in the forest, I heard notes climbing a scale, probably a Swainson's thrush. Twilight dimmed the river and day yielded to evening.

I climbed out of the Kalama and started looking around for the Coke machine, which was nowhere to be found.

You can lose the self in fly fishing. But the self is always waiting for you when you return. Fishing cleanses the spirit and frees you from some of your bonds, but only when you're standing in the river. Put away the rod and the old problems, fears, and uncertainties will be waiting for you when you get back. I felt an acute need to keep on moving. And so I drove down into California, just in time to chase a run of half-pounder steelhead in the Klamath River. The river was full of deep pools, gleaming bronze rocks, and sparkling riffles. I was a little disappointed in these half-pounders, a euphemism for immature steelhead that have come back after less than a year at sea; half-pounders weigh on average between one to three or four pounds. They could be viewed as either very large trout or very small steelhead—nothing like my experience on the Umpqua and Kalama. An angler told me I would have to come up here in winter for the big steelhead. That's when they passed through the Klamath to swim up into the turkey vulture canyons of the Trinity River.

I dropped into the volcano country around Shasta. I wanted to explore the canyon of the McCloud River deep in its remote conifer forest. I almost broke the axle of my car on a dirt road scarred by ruts and frost heaves. But I was treated to a beautiful view of Mount Shasta's volcanic cone floating over the trees. The conifer forest spread up the canyon in many shades of summertime, and the packed greenery forced the breath out of my lungs.

At first I couldn't see the river through the trees. Yet the forest sounded as if something was rising from beneath it, an unending and unyielding tone. The pine trees opened and suddenly the McCloud River was there, flowing dark green and turquoise gray with a mineral cloudiness. The bluish tint was peculiar to the McCloud and said to come from volcanic ash and glacial silt from the drainage of Mount Shasta. The river seemed alert, filled with spring bubblings, musical flutings, and a pouring sound, and it looked like sheer energy in the sunlight.

The water was cold and a little high but very fishable. It was full of boulders, riffles, and pocket water. The river was once the southernmost range for Dolly Varden trout, but these were now extinct in the McCloud.

It was a peculiar river, too. William Randolph Hearst once kept a fairy-tale castle hidden deep in the woods upriver. Hearst was San Francisco's dark lord of yellow journalism. ("You provide the pictures, I'll provide the war," Hearst told the artist Frederic Remington on the eve of the Spanish-American conflict.) By the 1920s Hearst had acquired through inheritance a family estate of some sixty-seven thousand acres of secluded virgin pine forest in the canyon of the upper McCloud River. This Hearst family holding put seven miles of river completely off limits to the public.

The Chief, as he was known to his troops, hired the services of the renowned Berkeley architect Bernard Maybeck to build a Teutonic fairyland on the banks of the McCloud, and the Bavarian village of stone and timber castles known as Wyntoon stands to this day, along with San Simeon on the California coast, as one of Hearst's monuments to himself.

Fearing that the Japanese might shell San Simeon (as if the Japanese navy had nothing more important to do during World War II), the aging Hearst holed up in Wyntoon during the war. Hearst's young mistress, the film actress Marion Davies, missed the parties and gaiety of San Simeon, and tried to break up the monotony and seclusion of Wyntoon with endless games of backgammon. (Think of the forlorn heroine in *Citizen Kane* sadly assembling her jigsaw puzzles.) Marion Davies called Wyntoon "Spittoon."

But Hearst considered it to be the acme of nature, and—taking inspiration from the sound of the McCloud River—he wrote a poem to the "riotous river," likening it to the riddle of existence or some such thing. The *San Francisco Examiner* duly punished its readers by publishing the poem on the op-ed page as an annual rite of torture.

While the Chief was alive, not a single pine tree on the estate was allowed to be cut down. But upon his death the acreage began to undergo gradual logging to help the Hearst Corporation pay taxes and continue the upkeep of the estate. Unlike San

Simeon, Wyntoon is not open to the public. When a commercial rafter tried to get a permit to operate on the McCloud in the seven-mile section that flowed past the Hearst estate, the family put the kibosh on the permit by refusing to allow rescue crews the right to cross private property in the event of an emergency. Newspapers that were not part of the Hearst chain had a field day covering the legal battle; Dean Munroe, the rafter, came off as a kind of deep-woods Orson Welles, his kayak Rosebud.

If I couldn't fish on the Hearst estate, at least I could fish here on the McCloud, in its remoter and much-harder-to-reach lower canyon. I waded into the river, armed with a light trout rod. The current grabbed hard at my waders. It created something like a vacuum around my legs, and the gravel slid under my boots. The blue tint from volcanic ash and the reflection of pine trees had given the water a gorgeous tinge. The river split apart at rocks and frothed lightly while running out of sight into submerged rock gardens.

I flexed the rod a few times, watching the tightly controlled arcs and loops of my casts. Ladybug Creek entered the river nearby, and its pool held wild trout that sipped insects washed down by the creek. A spilling sound came out of the mouth of the creek. Ladybug was the boundary of the Nature Conservancy preserve. From here downstream it was catch-and-release fishing.

I heard a much different sound, a sound apart from the splashing water, and I froze. A rooting and snuffling noise was coming out of the underbrush nearby. I stared hard into the shrubbery. The sound was unmistakable—a bear, or so I thought. The Mc-Cloud is one of the best places in northern California to stumble upon black bears. They've been known to make splashy crossings in the river only a few feet away from astonished fly fishermen.

I continued fishing, but my attention was drawn hard to the opposite bank where I had heard the noise. I could feel eyes upon me in the canyon.

There was a sharp tug on my rod and my focus returned to the river. The limber switch in my hand bent under the weight of a struggling trout. The rod bowed in the middle and I held it high, maintaining a delicate tension. All thoughts of the bear disappeared. The rod had a wonderful aliveness and spring to it. The line pulled, the rod jerked and pulsed, and the trout leapt out of the water. I lowered the rod tip to ease the strain on the leader. The rod jumped and its tip dipped once again toward the water. The trout was heavy in the current. I put pressure on the line, the rod bending, and brought the trout to me against the current. Holding the rod high over my head, I eased the trout toward the bank. It pumped and pumped, its head forced above the waterline.

I landed my trout. It was a two-pound rainbow, all dripping iridescence, with a darkly spotted dorsal and reddish lateral stripes turning to violet. It struggled in my hand. I knew that the cold trout was an archetype. The McCloud River was famous for producing one of the finest strains of wild trout that has ever existed.

In the late nineteenth century eggs taken from the McCloud River strain of rainbows (*Salmo shasta*) were used to stock streams in the eastern United States and in Europe. All the rainbow trout I had caught back East were descended from McCloud River fish. I looked at my shimmering trout, a trout so superior that it had been put out to stud, so to speak.

I eased the rosy trout back into the river. It held steady a moment then, realizing it was free, disappeared into the underwater luminance of the stream bottom.

The spilling sound continued to come from under the trees where Ladybug Creek frothed into the river. Beneath this sound was the single unending tone made up of all the different sounds in the canyon. The river drained through shadows under the pines and changed to brighter glints in the sunlight. The canyon was unconscious of its own beauty. I thought of how the fundamental quality of northern California must reside in such places.

It was a beautiful river and it will be inside me until I am dead. Some rivers I'd see again; others would flow only in my head. But in my mind they would run cold and clear and I would see them as I now saw the McCloud. I would know the weight and color of the river all my days. In a sense, I was now its owner. It had made me richer than a Hearst, more powerful than Citizen Kane.

There were spring creeks to explore in Shasta's volcano country. The best was Hat Creek, one of the most famous trout streams in the West. Hat Creek is for all practical purposes the lower half of the Rising River. Rising River is a relatively short spring creek draining a pristine marsh fed by ground springs hidden under volcanic rock. The clean water percolating up from the lava beds nourishes enormous brown trout, the kind that Bing Crosby used to catch on expensive split-bamboo fly rods on his ranch on the Rising River. The old Crosby ranch is now in the hands of Clint Eastwood.

Upper Hat Creek unwinds through the volcanic dumpings of Mount Lassen, where it drains a lumpy, thinly forested plateau. In its upper stretches it's much like any ordinary creek. And then a funny thing happens as it joins up with the Rising River. The Rising transforms Hat Creek from a tumbling mountain brook into a glassy chalkstream. Just below the junction of the two streams, the rich springhead flows created by the Rising River get rerouted. At the Cassel Forebay, Hat Creek is channeled into a diversion canal that leads down to the Hat Number One powerhouse, a generating station maintained by the Pacific Gas & Electric Company. The powerhouse dumps its outflow into an impoundment known as Baum Lake, and Baum's outflow is then shunted around Hat Creek (which by this time has been reduced to a mere trickle) and piped into the Hat Number Two powerhouse, where it generates more electricity. From there the water is discharged into Lower Hat Creek, or what has come to be known as the trophy-trout section—my destination.

The problem with Hat Creek was that it was as crowded as it was famous. The sight of all those fly fishermen in the creek playing with their flies made me want to jump back into the car and drive away. The bank just below the Hat Number Two powerhouse resembled the parking lot of a particularly disreputable roadhouse. Transformer lines that had been strung above a popular fishing riffle made a sound like beavers chewing the watershed.

I hiked half a mile downstream to escape the crowds. This was more like it. Blackbirds whistled in the cattails, and horses grazed behind corrals where bankside meadows rolled away toward sagebrush and soft chalky bluffs. The water was polished windowpane, the wide transparent creek loaded with fat trout that—I was soon to discover—were almost impossible to catch. The pools and slicks were absolutely clear, and under the bright sky the sand-and-gravel bottom was translucent.

Swarms of pale morning duns and even smaller *Baetis* whirled in mating dances above the creek, with spent and egg-laying mayflies dropping back to its surface. I dropped my artificial like a living insect onto the glassy tongues of water. After what seemed an eternity of refining my casts, lengthening my leader, and downsizing my flies, so to speak, I finally took a fifteen-inch rainbow in a lovely, swirling surprise.

This was volcano country, and I was offered distant glimpses of Mount Lassen and, somewhat farther away, Mount Shasta to occupy my time when I wasn't catching trout. Lassen is the southernmost in a series of huge volcanic cinder cones that line up to the Canadian border. Together these volcanoes—Lassen, Shasta, Hood, St. Helens, Adams, Rainier—are part of the most active volcano range in the contiguous United States. The double cone of Shasta was certainly in a class with Mount Fuji or Kilimanjaro. The pale outlines of Shasta and Lassen glimpsed in the distances made me think of Hokusai's pictures of the floating world.

By evening large stoneflies began falling in the riffle section of the creek below the powerhouse, where the meadow heads, but the trout were ignoring them. And then small caddisflies began falling on the water in much greater numbers than the stoneflies, and it seemed as if every trout in the river was suddenly rising at once. I managed to land three brown trout in the water just below the riffle. And I was oblivious to the crowds of fishermen around me.

Hat Creek drained its black mountain meadow under starlight. What a view there was inside that darkness. The creek pulled in a long, sinuous coil of liquid and energy, holding tiny points and glints of the night sky, empty and mindless of its beauty.

I spent the night at one of the forest service campsites on upper Hat Creek. There were no movie stars in the campground. I was surrounded by vacationing families and retirees in Winnebagos. Up here people worked in the sawmills or came from Redding, the big Sacramento hub town.

My neighbor was an elderly retiree who, from the looks of things, had set up his lawn chair in front of his Winnebago and not moved all day. He told me he'd seen Clint Eastwood fly over the creek in a helicopter.

"Clint doesn't fish," my neighbor explained. "He just likes to spend time up here enjoying nature."

I drove on to Yellow Creek, where Beefmaster cattle grazed behind split-cedar fences. I didn't know how Yellow Creek got its name. Perhaps from the way the meadow soaked up the sunlight. Or perhaps from the yellowish clay on the creek bottom. Or the yellow pines that fringed the valley. More likely, gold miners named Yellow Creek after a strike. And called the valley Humbug after it went bust.

It was early afternoon, and the meadow carried the whisper of hot wind in the wild grass. It was too bright and hot for bugs to be coming off the meadow stream. I could see down to the streambed, where brown and green weeds shifted and trailed in the water. The spring-fed creek was transparent, without the faint cloudiness the water sometimes took on when cows, owned by the Dye Creek Cattle Company, gathered at the headwaters to drink. The fence of hand-split cedar rails had been erected in the meadow to keep cattle from trampling the banks. But upstream, in the headwater, cattle grazed and freely watered there twice a day. The herd of Beefmasters stood at more than five hundred head.

The cattle grazed in Humbug Valley on a great spread of pasture owned by the utility giant Pacific Gas & Electric. The utility company was selling off some of its timber here, cutting down tree shade on the edge of the meadow. The stumps made me think of pine trees recently blue-painted for sawing near lower Hat Creek. The utility bought the pasture land around Yellow Creek many years ago, when there had been some ill-conceived talk about drowning the beautiful little valley under a reservoir.

Pioneers planted brown trout in Yellow Creek in the nineteenth century, and the large size of those fish at one time made the creek famous. Now, however, the brown trout were said to be smaller.

Because it was so hot, I waited until evening to fish. The pine forest gathered light, seeded darkness. In the meadow, trout rings appeared one by one in the lazy twists of the creek. I tried to secure a clinch knot in the fading light. Upstream, another angler gazed into his fly box, picking at it daintily as if it held sleeping butterflies that he didn't want to wake.

The creek was narrow and certainly not deep. My caddis rode high, and when a small brown trout rose to it, I struck and missed. I fumbled around and blew some more casts, until finally I had the line unrolling and sailing out properly. A trout rose inches from my fly. And another. Bastard! Once again my line unfurled and floated out over the creek, the leader settling down as lightly as a feather. This time when a trout rose, my rod bent under a weight that I swear felt as heavy as a whiskey bottle. But I never got a look at that trout, because my leader broke.

The next morning I was driving into the heart of gold country, on the western slope of the Sierras, where the rivers pour out of canyon labyrinths. I was thinking of giant sequoias and high waterfalls.

At the entrance to Yosemite I gazed into John Muir's Range of Light. Here was the very view of the valley on which Ansel Adams opened his f-stops: the dancing waters of the Merced River; the sheared face of Half Dome; Yosemite Falls plunging in a white jet of negative ions. Sunshine bathed peaceful Stoneman Meadow, where years before hippies had battled park rangers in a famous riot. At Camp Six I saw the tents, sleeping bags, and rucksacks of the rock-climbing tribe, those "angels of light" scaling El Capitan. And here was something not depicted on my Sierra Club photo calendar—a score or more of retail liquor outlets and a Los Angeles haze over the valley.

Like any good tourist, I took in the views from Glacier Point. And where the trail heads at Tuolumne Meadows I set out into the backcountry for remote Waterwheel Falls. Foaming rapids heaved over stones, flinging fountains of mist into the gorge. I watched the tremendous falls splashing and spraying against the granite, its cascades leaping from one level to the next, dropping through space, dissolving into vapor.

Leaving the park late in the afternoon, I headed eastward on Tioga Road, bound for the highest paved mountain pass in California. The ascent up the heavily forested westward slope of the

Sierra Nevada, its height great but angle gradual, did little to prepare me for what came next.

From the roof of California I gazed down at one of the most exhilarating panoramas in the West. Below lay one of the steepest descents on the planet. The eastern escarpment of the Sierra Nevada plunged dramatically into a sage-covered basin. What lay beyond was empty and austere. Here was a vast acreage set down between the Sierra Nevada crest and the White-Inyo Mountains, stretching out to Nevada, an unspoiled landscape of dramatic contrasts and remarkable beauty, of subtlety and extremes. Desert wastes shone beyond phantom hills. Dead Mono Lake lay like a blue mirage in a buff landscape. Graying sagebrush and corkscrew junipers dotted the hills and flats.

I was staring down into an American outback, a vast rain shadow on the continent, an area as remote and desolate as any in the country. There was something in the vast and arid landscape that resisted my knowing it. Each hour the desert light produced a different tone and color. Distances ran out endlessly to the horizons. I was baffled by the scale, the immensity, the great massive fact of the basin.

I descended to the valley floor. Shadows lengthened a hundred feet and more as evening stole across sagebrush hills. In the western sky, the evening star shone above the great wall of the Sierra Nevada.

In the sagebrush flats there wound a spring creek as perfectly formed as any I had ever seen; trout rings appeared in the serpentine bends. I fished into the deep blackness of a mountain night.

What a view. More stars than I had seen since those nights in Jackson Hole, glimmering with a diamond brilliance over the desert. Starlight shining in the empty blackness of outer space. It was among the most glorious night skies I had ever witnessed. I wasn't so much looking at it as beholding it. I *beheld* our universe.

And so I explored the lonesome California outback, the huge back of beyond. I fished desert spring creeks, lush riparian ribbons that emerged from the sagebrush as if from some miracle of hydraulics. I traveled to remote outposts and discovered desert seeps, dry lake beds, and poison springs; I traveled up high mountain passes toward fragrant evergreen forests and hanging valleys, blinding glacier fields, and sapphire lakes. I listened to the breathing and whispering of aspens in the high country, and I caught golden trout in the ultraviolet zone. I counted rosy dawns and lilac twilights and felt the stealthy shifting of light and silhouette across the long shadow valleys.

Dawn came to the Sierra Nevada. The eastern sky appeared as a rosy band on the horizon, paling to green beneath a brightening dome. I watched for some minutes, my eyes fixed on the horizon, my patience rewarded. The light broke over the mountains, its sun too painful to look at directly.

On the western side of the valley the land rolled once, a ridge of foothills and sagebrush, and then in a single surge rose ten thousand feet. Viewed from down here in the basin, the snow-capped peaks of the Sierra Nevada were fired a rose color by the sun. As the fireball lifted off the horizon, the pink reflection on the snow spread downward over the mountain face, and soon the range was glowing.

The foothills were transforming themselves, with just enough light on them to reveal rock gullies and bunched sagebrush. I could just make out the black silhouettes of horses in a nearby corral. I stared out over the dry outback as the desert basin materialized beyond the sagebrush hills. The landscape was so vast that it unsettled me, suggesting a lack of limits.

I could see the Sweetwater Mountains to the north, and to the east the Bodie Hills. Over to my right were an abandoned bunkhouse and an old stockman's shed preserved in dryness. The old rancher was gone. He had always been a part of the land, more joined to it as he grew older, and when he went into his grave he became the land.

Sagebrush and juniper threw long shadows on the ground. I headed out on foot across the sagebrush flat. In the high, thin air, the morning light was a tinted transparency, golden toward the sun, smoky blue in the shadows of the hills. The Sierras appeared as bold as galleons under full sail. The blowing clouds caused the peaks to resemble an armada passing against the sky. The old snowpack was dazzling atop the crest. Mountains and basin were touched by the golden tint of desert air, and the shadows on the mountains stood out hard and true. In the clean light of morning, each angle and declivity in the Sierra wall held a shadow as sharp and real as the rock itself.

The scent of sagebrush brought the basin right up into my nostrils. The air was very dry. In the early light the sage was a blend of greens, blues, and silvers mixing into a kind of desert aquamarine. The dark, feathery roots rose up into aromatic clusters concealing tiny purple blossoms, and when I crushed a few leaves between my fingers, I released the sharp and pungent odor of the desert.

The river had another scent, a fresh willowy one. The East Walker wended its way between banks of sedge, rabbitbrush, and coyote willow, its shining bends holding the desert basin in freshwater reflection. Birds chirped in rapid chorales along the banks. The river flowed slowly, steadily, the light on its bottom a richly tannic whiskey gold. The river looked young because it was young, renewing itself moment by moment.

At one widening bend the river shifted direction smoothly, the current moving faster on the outside curve, more slowly nearer the shallow bar. A seam formed between the slower and faster currents, and the erosion was noticeable on the farther bank. My eyes followed the changing curve as the river flowed eastward into the desert basin toward Nevada. The depth of the river changed from moment to moment. In the shallows the transparency increased; light seemed to vibrate on the water's surface membrane. Looking down at river stones through the light's refraction, the stones appeared to be wavering within a clear gel, yet they still appeared sharp and remarkably distinct. The effect was a little like looking at an object distorted by a magnifying glass. When I plucked a stone from the water it appeared to shrink in my hand as it dried.

I didn't care to rush things. I went over my tackle carefully—the limber rod joined at the ferrule, the clinched knots, the tubular wormlike fly at the end of my leader—before stepping into the stream.

The water was cold and the gravel crunched under my wading boots. I experienced a familiar pleasure as the soles of my boots felt for the bottom and the river slid under them. Wading a stream is one of the most satisfying feelings I know. The water never rose higher than my thighs, yet it pulled at my legs, making it difficult to cross. At the deepest part, near midstream, I had to brace my legs apart and lean into the current to stay upright.

I positioned myself and made a few false casts; the line weaving back and forth with the old familiar rhythm made me feel as if I were writing my signature on the air. A few small, dark caddisflies fluttered around, riding the currents and floating up into the air.

But I saw no telltale trout rings. Something must have been going on near the bottom that held the attention of the trout. The river flowed by at a moderate pace, and the surface remained smooth and fairly unbroken.

My lure drifted near the bottom. There was a small tug at the end of my line and I pulled it taut. Holding the rod against the current, I stripped in line with my left hand. The rod bent slightly, the tip jouncing. It was a small trout, pumping against the rod, against the tension in the line that held the fish in place. I brought the trout to the surface and watched it thump excitedly in the water. A rainbow, its sides flashed in the sun. Its back was a mottling of black-and-olive camouflage. I leaned over and with my left hand lifted the little trout completely out of the water. Tucking the rod under my right arm, I gently removed the fly from the trout's upper lip and set it back in the water.

I waded downstream, casting. The current carried the fly under the water, under the early-morning shadows of willow branches lining the river. The line tapped and I set the hook. A trout pulled hard and drew line out toward the middle of the river. This was a much larger trout. I got the fish on the reel quickly and held it steady at midstream. The fish thumped in the water against the vibrancy of the rod. I maneuvered it into the shallows, fifteen inches of flipping and splashing brown trout. Leaning over, I unfastened the hook without touching the trout. It fled with a splash of its tail.

I moved along through the shallows, casting, and a third trout tapped on my line. The tip twitched, the rod dipped low toward the water, and I pulled up on the trout. The rod jerked and bent and I could feel the fish through the living spring of the rod. The trout ran downstream and flashed near the surface but didn't jump. Through the rod's vibration, I could feel the trout circling. I drew on the jerking, pumping rod, forcing the trout to the surface. Walking toward the bank, rod held high, I reeled in line slowly, pleased by the fish's heaviness. My leader strained as it slid up into the rod guides. I brought a tiring brown trout onto the bank and let it go.

Sitting down on the bank, I checked my tackle. All was secure. That was a particularly good trout. The sun felt warm on the back of my neck. Ahead the river narrowed as it wound into a steep valley of rough rounded hills. The rocks rising up from the sagebrush terrace seemed designed for stress. This was earthquake country, after all.

I stood up, water running down my waders and out of my wading boots. The boots made a squishing sound as I walked along the bank. The river, shining and smooth, curved around a bend that rose up into a solid terrace of sagebrush. I could see the channel, its color deepening, carving a rut out of the bank. I waded back into the river, moving downstream, aided by the steady push of current.

I was using a weighted, sinking leader to get the fly down deep. That's where the largest brown trout in the river must be feeding.

Early in the twentieth century anglers from as far away as Montana used to make the long trip in their tin lizzies just to fish for the brown trout here. Those must have been some trout. Few Montanans make the trip anymore. Nowadays everyone goes to Montana to fish.

There was a long tug on my line and when I brought it taut the rod came alive, convulsing in my hand. The line tightened dangerously, the rod bending double, and the reel let loose a mechanical squawk. I palmed the reel hard and stopped the ratcheting sound. The line tightened into a sudden hardness, and at a spot much farther downstream than I would have guessed a large trout flipped backward out of the water, landing with a heavy splash. And then the line started pulling off the reel again in spurts.

The rod was alive and pumping against the heavy trout. I sloshed backward, working the trout upstream. The rod felt springy and animate, jerking and recovering, absorbing the trout's fight. The limber stick was charged with all of the trout's fighting qualities. I stumbled through the shallows after it.

Two or three times I tried to work the trout toward me, always keeping the bank at my back, only to have the fish surge away when it got a look at me. I moved backward slowly, carefully, the rod held high above my head. The rod bent and strained under the heaviness of the fish; its dark dorsal surface was now flashing above water.

The trout's head came out of the water and I could see the fly embedded in the large undershot jaw. I was aware of several

things at once. The feeling of living weight on the end of my line.
The wind kicking up over the basin, wrinkling the surface of the
river. One two three four small birds flying out of the willows.
slid the large trout onto the bank. It was extravagantly marked
with black spottings all over its heavy back, its tail thick and solid.
I paused to recover my breath, my hands shaking slightly. Jesus,
hadn't taken a brown trout that large in some years. I released the
fish, first making sure it was steady enough to swim away under
its own strength.

The wind was kicking up dust devils in the sagebrush and the
clouds were racing across the sky. It would blow hard for the remainder of the day. It did that kind of thing out here often. Out
here the wind was as much a part of things as the sagebrush and
the sky. Looking up at the serrated edges of the Sierra Nevada,
was reminded once again how suited I was to the fishing life.

The season was at its hottest, and I could feel the pull of the cool
Pacific on the other side of the mountains. They say that once you
have lived beside an ocean you are not content to live anywhere
else. I drove back over the Sierras and down into the hot lettuce
fields of the Salinas Valley. This was Steinbeck country, and from
coastal mountains covered in madrone I glimpsed the Pacific
shining at the edge of the continent.

At Big Sur the ice fringe plants marked the end of the land.
Before the fog burned off, an endless expanse of cotton floated

188

over the ocean. On the beach, sanderlings darted by, light flashing off white underwings. The surf frothed and poured over miles of rocks, sending up a muffled roar. Emerald cliffs dropped abruptly into the blue ocean. Long streamers of kelp rose and fell in green illuminated waves. Deep canyons emptied onto beaches and disappeared behind ragged, crumbling headlands. There were streams hidden back there under cascades of cliffside vegetation, tiny trout creeks disappearing into jungles of poison oak. At night the fog rolled back in, streaming in rags through the redwoods. In cabins under the trees, the earthy vapor of bay leaf and Scotch broom mixed with the faintly sour odor of redwood shakes. In the morning the redwood trunks would be steaming in the sunshine.

Sea lions barked on empty beaches. Thick forests rose steeply into Pacific fogs. Green hills emerged under glaucous cloud layers. And at dusk the final rays of sunlight dissolved in ocean foam.

Once, on the Carmel Highlands overlooking the Pacific, I saw the fabled green flash of sunset for the first time. I had been watching for this rare atmospheric event for years. The air was crystalline, with no fog over the ocean. The Pacific met the land in a sweep of marine brilliance. I stared westward across unbroken ridges of Monterey pine and cypress as the sun sank into the Pacific. At the very moment the sun disappeared below the horizon, it seemed to extinguish itself in the water, and there was an exquisite puff of emerald, the final color of the dying sun.

At Santa Cruz, a beach-and-surf town, the ocean was a blue upwelling. Boats went out onto Monterey Bay in search of schooling salmon. I joined some other fishermen to catch olive rockfish on fly rods, pulling them out of the living kelp beds. Coming ashore, a radiant sunset light fell on radish blooms along farm roads, on fields of mustard and thistles.

Farther up the coast at Pescadero, the surf was alive with cabezon and eels. Windswept coves yielded limpets and sea urchins. Riding down the seaward side of the mountains, through the fog and redwoods, past the Homer Ranch and the tiny town of La Honda, I emerged from second-growth redwood groves into rolling, treeless pastures that ended in a sweep of artichoke fields by the sea. The violet marshland floodplain along Pescadero Creek was filled with white egrets. A pebbled beach nearby was a color between gray and onyx, and the ocean swept in each day to inlay the rocks with shells, turban snails, and purple rock crabs. I fished for rockfish in kelp beds that helped hold the surf in shape and watched sea lions playing in the foamy green light of the waves.

One evening, watching a long line of sunset combers, the desire to travel and fish seemed to go out of me like a sigh. After fifteen weeks of trout rivers, and these final days on lonesome Pacific beaches, I was more than ready to listen to good jazz in smoky clubs, eat in Chinatown noodle joints, and hit the bars along the Barbary Coast. I wanted to hear the slap of dice cups on wood and listen to the atonal moaning of foghorns on San Francisco Bay.

I decided at that moment that my trip was over. I liked this coast and these mountains. I liked the look and feel of northern California. I liked the Sierra Nevada and the redwood forests and the magnificent coast. I decided it was time to find a place to live and line up a job. Although my money had by no means run out, I felt it was time to get back to work anyway, resume my interrupted career, and maybe write a book. I had satisfied the urge to fish, at least for the time being. I had found out I didn't need a year after all; just a season. I had fulfilled my deepest needs and found my bliss. I had been healed from whatever it was that had been ailing me. At least for the time being. I had cured my boredom, created opportunities to fish, and found a better place to live. More important, I had acted on my desires. Now it was time to get back to real life and do the work of a writer.

We are most alive when we live in close harmony with nature. But as refreshing as nature by itself can be, it alone can never be enough. Along with nature's timelessness must go an equal concern with temporal realities if we are to live fully engaged in the world. If fishing were merely an escape, this would have been nothing but a pleasant vacation. But fishing is a way of feeling things more keenly and being more alert to life, and from the vantage of a stream I sometimes discover things that I did not know before. One of the greatest rewards of travel is to return home. Now I had a new home to come back to. All trips have a beginning and an end, but this time it had come down to something more. In a way, this trip had turned into my life.

I reached San Francisco the next night. The city was lit up like a luxury liner, its running lights burning in the fog. The bridges, with their moving streams of traffic, appeared as gleaming necklaces strung across the bay. Deep-sea freighters passed under the Golden Gate, and the windowpanes in the Berkeley Hills seemed to be reflecting fire. Richmond rose up from its lagoon of black lacquer, glowing out of a bed of chemical and acid mist. Who could believe a city could be so bewitching? Sounds carried on the salt-misty night: the signal beeps of vessels and tugs out on the bay, the low diaphones of foghorns. I watched the velvet sea fog from a friend's apartment on Russian Hill, and drank in Chinatown bars with names like Li Po, Buddha, and Red's Place.

An entire summer. I had seen rivers in their surviving and squandered glory, and I had gained access to things outside and within myself. Such a unity of landscape, and on such a grand scale. I was reminded of who we are as a people, and what we may someday become. I settled in for a long stay.

Nine

WHERE I LIVED,
AND WHAT I LIVED FOR

*I*n northern California steelhead fishing is exclusively a winter proposition. And each winter in those years when I was settling into my new home, I would try to make at least one trip up to the north coast to treat what had become a very serious steelhead jones.

Rainy winters in San Francisco had me longing to get out of town. For one thing, someone or something was changing the music out on the bay. The low, mysterious diaphones of the old-fashioned foghorns were competing with the beeps and peanut whistles of newer electronic models. San Francisco was famous for the sound of its foghorns, but there was little romance or resonance in these new tones.

Beginning sometime in autumn I would fish the nearby Russian River. Occasionally the river would host a fairly decent run of salmon and steelhead. As usual, fall alchemized the landscape, painting vine maples and poplars a scintillant orange and old gold. Along the river, the redwood groves filled with warm haze and low-angle sunlight. Down in the valley, grapevines reddened like returning salmon.

One darkly overcast morning I found myself fishing the Cassini Ranch water. The pools were like transparent lenses, the water a mysterious black-and-green reflection. I had not seen the Russian River this low and clear before. It was a revelation. A salmon showed itself by rolling in the perfectly still water at Watson's Log. Concentric circles spread out from where the great fish had rolled on the surface. A few raindrops made their own smaller circles on the water. What I remember mostly from that day was the tranquillity, the dark redwoods rising steeply off the north bank, the grand silence before the rainfall.

I fished for hatchery kings and the steelhead that later followed them into the Russian River. The river was about an hour and a half from San Francisco, a convenient day trip. By early autumn the Russian would still be low and clear, sliding past vineyards, orchards, and river towns before easing its way past the dairy farms and sheep ranches that bordered the final tidal stretches. The lower pools were deep and quiescent, shaded by pockets of second-growth redwoods mixed with a few Douglas firs. Standing in the river, you might look up at a high evergreen tilting out over the pool and feel a momentary vertigo. A pair of minks might poke their heads from niches and crevices along the steep rocky banks and scamper among downed logs, wholly unconcerned with the presence of fishermen. Mallards exploded from the water and beat their wings upriver. The current passed calmly beneath the watchful gaze of turkey vultures floating on updrafts or roosting on high branches.

I fished the Austin Riffle, at Neeley's Beach, and in the big pool at Guerneville. One day, as municipal workers were removing a flashboard dam, I counted two dozen king salmon leaping the artificial falls created by the loosened planks. "River towns are winged towns," said Henry David Thoreau.

One evening I found myself at a place called the Bohemian Pool. Across the river sat a vast acreage of redwoods known as Bohemian Grove, a private reserve said to contain more trip-wire security devices than even the White House. I had heard much about Bohemian Grove, little of it good. Membership in the Bohemian Club was made up of the wealthiest and most powerful white capitalist males in America (there was an eighteen-year waiting list), and its redwood grove had been the playground of every Republican president since Calvin Coolidge. Each July the club would hold a summer jamboree under the redwoods. Guests drank heavily, listened to speeches, mingled with the likes of Henry Kissinger and Walter Cronkite, dressed up for the costume pageant, and occasionally, rumor had it, visited the hookers working the motels across the river. Once the good old boys' club had been sued for prohibiting the fair sex on its grounds. In defending its policy of hiring only male waiters, lawyers for Bohemian Grove had argued in court that many of the male guests frequently walked about in the woods *au naturel.*

I was a little surprised to see salmon in the Bohemian Pool. I could only make them out imperfectly in the failing light, their underwater bodies as gray as the dusk. It was heartbreaking to see how the salmon held out against the tragedy of the river. They had come so far only to arrive at this terribly abused place, and now they were parked in a pool across from a rich man's club. I had never seen creatures look so solemn and purposeful.

Sometime after Thanksgiving a line of weak winter storms might begin bearing down on the coast. And it was then that I would start thinking seriously about Gualala. The Gualala River is a priceless little steelhead stream flowing out of the Coast Ranges about a hundred miles north of San Francisco. Once a week I might make a telephone call up north to ask if the river was in fishable shape. And each week I would get the same answer: not yet. The Gualala River wouldn't be ready until the first good storm of winter blew out its sandbar at the beach. Around Christmas I would get the news I longed to hear.

Few things made me happier than a trip up to Gualala for steelhead. The ride up the wild north coast was always fascinating; the view of the abrupt headlands filled me with the drama of being alive.

I called a friend in San Francisco and asked him if he was interested in accompanying me for a few days. Hal was the person who had first introduced me to the Gualala River not long after I moved to California. He could be eccentric and touchy, but he had fishing in his heart. In fact, Hal had such a passion for fishing that I was astonished to learn that he had never once purchased a California fishing license. He called this civil disobedience. "Do you know why there are so many damn carp and squawfish in the Russian River?" Hal asked me once. "It's because the California Department of Fish and Game hasn't lifted a finger to help them."

I figured Hal would be eager to escape a city whose indignities he complained of daily. My friend lived in an imaginary San Franciso of crime, libertinism, and runaway cable cars, a place where if the crack didn't kill you, the California cuisine would. He once complained to me that buggery had long ago replaced Rice-a-Roni as the San Francisco treat.

When I broached the idea of a road trip, Hal said he would gladly accompany me to Gualala if I would throw in the Eel and Smith rivers, too. He said he was feeling an acute vascular need to nail a steelhead.

From our elevated vantage point on the Highway 1 bridge, we looked down upon a short coastal river flowing out of a redwood canyon. The damp redwood grove looked peaceful, and the river pools were the soft green color California steelhead anglers often dream about.

In the distance I could see three fly fishermen standing in the tailout of Miner Hole. Hal promptly announced that there were too many frigging people on the river. For a moment I feared he would turn the pickup truck around in the middle of the bridge and drive back to San Francisco.

The redwood grove was full of winter light. Even at noon the sun remained low in the sky. There was a hush in the grove, blond light on the river. Fronds of licorice fern clung to bare hardwood limbs. Slender trunks of bay laurels struggled horizontally toward patches of sunlight or bent under their own top-heavy foliage. I thought of how sunshine filtering down into a redwood grove always seems best the day after a winter rain, as shafts of light slant into condensing ground vapors.

The air hung still above the canyon, almost windless. I detected a fragrant mixture of wet river scents. Steep banks of redwood lent definition to broad green pools, their currents hardly noticeable. Voices carried far over the water, or from the campground hidden behind the trees. In the distance a chain saw whined. The day was serene, a mild sixty degrees.

We stepped into a pool that dimly reflected the redwoods rising off the bank. The afternoon sun slanted into deeper water and helped lighten the green color. We cast out and followed the progress of our lines downstream; white specks of foam and bubbles drifted by on a barely visible current. The motions of casting, the unrolling of line in the air, took on the feeling of ceremony. We waded out within inches of our wader tops as the casting rhythms set in. I couldn't help but envy Hal's perfect loops and immaculate turnovers. When we picked up line from the water, spray flew off in crystal droplets and mist.

An hour went by like this. The steelhead is said to be a fish of a thousand casts, and for me this was literally true. But nothing could beat a mild winter day on the California coast, with green water and December sun.

"How about it, Hal, does it get any better than this?" I asked.

"I wouldn't mind hearing a little Hardy music," my friend said, turning the handle on his reel.

Hal hadn't failed to notice that an angler downriver had a steelhead on his line. Hal often got a bit put out when someone was catching fish and he wasn't. He had a tendency to blame the lack of action on such things as barometric pressure or the company that manufactured his fly rod.

"If we get these casts out just a little farther," Hal said, "we'll be sitting pretty."

The afternoon slid by gradually, like the river. We fished Thompson's Hole a little way upstream, and Hal caught his steelhead, playing it expertly, as he always did, backing it carefully out of the water toward the sandbar. It was a henfish of seven pounds, and when he let the silvery trout go he shot me one of his patented smug looks.

We returned to the tailout of Miner Hole in time for the first shadows slipping into the water off the north bank. In the absence of direct sunlight the temperature had dropped by ten degrees. Hal said that fresh steelhead might be coming in on the rising tide, and he suggested we try Mill Bend.

In that late hour a light mist had begun to form over the river, and by the time we got downstream to the highway bridge we had stepped into a painting made of the colors of dusk and fog. In the gloom, the cliff overlooking Mill Bend posed a primordial mystery, with mosses and lichens forming a dull winter patchwork. What little light remained in the canyon reflected off the cliff face and was cold comfort to us down in the river.

With little more than half an hour of false light remaining, Hal suggested we walk the lagoon to see if ocean steelhead had slipped in over the sandbar. Gulls cried and a light sea breeze passed through twisted stands of cypress. I saw no boils on the calm surface of the lagoon. Twenty minutes after the sun set behind the offshore fog bank, the sky began to radiate a lemon afterglow. I wanted the sun to rise through the haze and repeat the day in reverse.

That night we paid a visit to the Gualala Hotel, a century-old saloon. It was something of a ritual of ours. Hal hit on the barmaid, telling her he was the original Ivory Snow baby, a pickup line I hadn't heard before. Gretchen, the bartender, told us a true story: "An old guy, a real mountain man, comes out of the woods.

He walks into the bar on a Saturday night, plops a hundred-dollar bill on the bar, and says, 'I want me a woman.' Linda—she's the weekend bartender—she tells him: 'I'm sorry, sir, we don't do that anymore.' " In the lobby of the hotel, I had seen a wonderful old photograph showing loggers standing on the front steps and the ladies upstairs leaning over the balcony.

I admired a pair of wild boars' heads mounted on the saloon wall, and a colossal steelhead over the doorway. There were vintage photographs on the wall showing Governor Earl Warren and Fred MacMurray displaying their catches.

Joe Panic used to own the bar. By most accounts he was a character. He'd been dead some years now. He was a sportsman, a lifelong bachelor, "a man's man," Gretchen called him. "He didn't see much point in having women around. He liked to fish and hunt. And he didn't care whether the place was open or not. He'd go fishing and close the bar."

Joe had a lot of Hollywood friends, like Fred MacMurray, who honeymooned at Gualala with his bride, June Haver, one winter steelhead season. MacMurray later brought Governor Earl Warren to Gualala to fish. Even at the turn of the twentieth century, the Gualala Hotel saloon had been a favorite watering hole of Jack London.

"Most of the old-timers are gone, or close to gone," Gretchen said. "Too many heart attacks and strokes. And people's drinking habits have changed. It's pretty sad compared to the way it used to be. We're not getting into fights and busting out windows anymore."

I thought of Joe Panic's coastal hills rich in game, the thick forests rising steeply out of winter fogs. Outside the warm and familiar tavern, the sea wind blew through stands of eucalyptus and the surf plunged beneath headlands toward the south. All up and down the broken hills, sheep ranches stood out above the Pacific like frontier outposts. You wondered how long it could all last.

Daybreak: The headlands loomed darkly to the south. A thin fog layer lay just offshore, invisible in the predawn light. Beyond the awesome boil of the Pacific breakers were giant rocks stained white by seabirds. The northwest wind curved around the sea cliffs, sculpting the cypress into expressive shapes. At the crunching surf line, wet sand was ground over and over, polished to a gleaming, satin finish by the tide.

The redwood groves lay a little farther inland, and in the false dawn they appeared much darker than the beach. The first settlers had found these coastal woodlands oppressive, even a little threatening. They cleared the land for homesteads, and timber companies wasted little time harvesting the trees for their wealth. The pools of the Gualala had been named after logging operations. Now the towering giants, the last of their kind on earth, have been confined largely to a few state and federal theme parks. The biggest tracts are farther north and spread out along the coast; the trees in the Gualala groves are secondary or tertiary growth.

The sound of the wind coming off the headlands was dampened by the grove, lost among the high branches of the evergreens. The path at my feet disappeared under the dark spires, and the blackness waiting for me inside felt particularly fertile.

I could sense the river beyond the trees, the current passing unseen. The air was wet and fragrant, the ground soft with conifer needles fallen onto hummocks of earth. Noble trunks rose in columns spaced out among the ferns, their black crowns invisible to me from the forest floor. Following the soft duff trail, I emerged from the gloom, coming out at last onto the wide gravel bar at the lower end of Miner Hole. Morning vapor rose off the water, laying a wreath upon the air.

I sat on a driftwood log and began to assemble my tackle. This was one of the best tidal pools in the river, a staging area for the anadromous fish. Steelhead fresh from the sea rested here, adjusting to their new environment. Perhaps the next rain would move them upstream. Some would veer off at the north fork; others would spread into the tributaries. Once in the headwater shallows, the steelhead would touch and shudder against one another, emptying themselves into the river gravel. Some wouldn't survive the spawning journey, and much could be made of that as a metaphor. I long ago concluded that I lived in a tragic but sacramental universe.

I had come a long way to learn how to do this. Stringing the rod, I felt an eerie rolling beneath my feet. A light shaking, traveling up from the gravel bar, entering my bones through the log I was sitting on. A tiny earthquake, not an uncommon thing in California. The woods began to creak, as if many little feet were pattering about in the forest. As a newcomer to the state, I had made an uneasy alliance with the ground. Did the steelhead feel it? I waited some minutes, expecting an aftershock. None followed.

The sky paled in the east. It was going to be another bright winter day. With the dawn, the canyon grew less abstract; the redwoods took on gradual definition. River stones gleamed on the gravel bar, and moss and ferns shone wetly. I could just make out the lower end of the big pool, and I imagined steelhead holding in the flow in servitude to their instinct.

The cold shock of water enveloped my waders. The fresh scent of the river and trees mingled together. I uncoiled line from my reel and worked it into the air. The river continued its slow glide in peace.

I cast and tried to visualize my fly sinking into the dimness. My breath steamed in the cold morning air. A thin yoke of sun was showing on the haze.

The Gualala River was typical of the shorter coastal streams. On one side was a curving gravel bar, on the other a steep canyon bank covered in redwoods and ferns. The current pressed against banks boxed in by streamside alders, and it bulged against rocks carpeted in winter mosses and yellowing lichens. The water was a soft chalky green, not quite emerald, recently freshened by a rain.

The canyon was beautiful, changing from mothlike to green in the sunlight. The distant wash of the sea could be heard beyond the forest. The haze would be burning off soon, and already the sky was showing itself as breakable eggshell.

Spray flew off the line with each cast, my turnovers fully extending. Ground vapors rose into hazy sunshine, the redwood grove radiant and filling with light. A mallard whirred overhead.

My sunken fly bumped into something and stopped in mid-drift. I pulled up smoothly on the rod and there was solid resistance, the unmistakable feeling of weight stirring to life. I set the hook sharply and a steelhead leapt out of the river. Twenty yards of line hummed off my reel.

My rod plunged and the steelhead leapt again, returning once more to the river with a powerful splash. The fish somersaulted back into the water, thrashed and bore downward. The rod plunged and recovered, and more line spun off the reel.

I followed the boil downstream, my reel surrendering line in spasms. The steelhead was out of the pool now, and I followed it into the glittering wrinkle in the shallow riffle, water streaming around my ankles. The steelhead thrashed madly in the shallows, straining, using the current to its advantage. I began to regain line.

My leader tested at ten-pound strength, so I would have to play this fish with a mixture of force and delicacy. I tried to hold the rod in such a way as to absorb shocks that might break the leader. The rod plunged and bucked, but I managed to retake line.

The steelhead circled deep, twisting, and I could see it flashing below. It swam a few yards and shook its head as I tried to pump and reel in. The steelhead strained deeply, but we both knew it was over.

As I slowly drew it to the surface, the fish began thrashing and floundering in desperation. I led its head toward the shallows. It gave a final swipe of its tail and turned on its side in defeat.

I reckoned this fish weighed seven or eight pounds, a beautiful steelhead, if perhaps a little below the average weight for the river. I pulled the fly gently from the corner of its jaw and tried to hold the steelhead upright in the current. It cast a small torpedo shadow on the sand bottom. The bright skin looked like a mixture of river transparency and metal alloy. I drew it gently back and forth in the current until the fish stopped teetering and its gills began to move regularly. When I saw that the steelhead could remain upright on its own, I let it go, and the fish pushed away for deeper water, disappearing altogether.

Below me lay several hundred yards of green water lined by alders. Beyond this stretch the river broadened into a sweeping bend where it passed under the highway bridge. In time I could work my way so far downstream that I would be able to glimpse the Pacific through the cliff cypress. Or I could fish upriver, back to Thompson's Hole. It was barely nine o'clock and the tide was coming in. The debate had never been fully resolved: fish the rising or falling tide? A rising tide gave steelhead a helpful push of water. But a falling tide allowed the river's scent to mingle with the ocean and stir the memories of returning steelhead waiting to enter the mouth.

That evening Hal and I paid particular attention to the weather report. A low-pressure system was lying off the coast, threatening to bring in a trough of wet air. I thought the drop in atmosphere might stir the fish, but Hal wanted to clear out in the morning for the Eel River.

The following morning we shared a rain-slick highway with a procession of logging trucks hauling first- and second-growth redwood bound for the sawmills. Their girths suggested that the trees had lived for centuries. A bumper sticker on a truck read: SAVE A LOGGER. KILL A SPOTTED OWL.

The hills rose steeply into thickening stands of redwood and Douglas fir. It rained harder as we dropped into the canyon of the Eel River. I gazed down into the deep and vaporous gorge. A ragged mist drifted in and out of the darkly forested mountains.

Below us, mossy boulders emerged from swirling green pools. Foaming creeks spilled out of the forest. Gravel bars lined the banks, and towering trees leaned dangerously from moss-covered cliffs. Fog spiraled out of the canyon toward the thickening clouds. "The blue mountains are constantly walking," wrote

Dogen, centuries ago. The poet Tu Fu said: "The state is destroyed, but the mountains and rivers survive."

We'd have to hurry if we wanted to get in any fishing on the Eel River, always the first river in northern California to muddy up after a rain. Already it was beginning to lose its greenish tint.

Because it has been so badly overlogged in its upper drainage, the Eel is notorious for staying unfishable for weeks. The upside of this, if any, is that the tremendous clouds of silt in the river protect ascending steelhead from fishermen.

Our pool below the redwood grove looked almost too deep to wade. I found a run I thought I could manage. "Go on," urged Hal. "It's not tragic to die doing what you love."

The light was pearly and the water a foamy green wash. I imagined steelhead holding steady in the current, or moving up the shallow edges of it, and I marveled at the navigational fix that had brought them from the ocean to this canyon. I had read that salmon and steelhead at sea find their way back to their birth rivers by following an infinitely arcing grid of low-voltage current created by the earth's magnetic field.

I looked up at the surrounding hills and thought about the chain saws. It pained me to think that the timber cut in northern California had recently been tripled so that the company that now owned Pacific Lumber could pay off its junk bond debts. More painful was the knowledge that Charles Hurwitz, the Texas corporate raider who had seized the northern California timber company in a hostile takeover, had worked out the details of the debt refinancing over a steelhead fishing trip with his bankers up on the Trinity River. The destruction of the watershed had been mapped out over a *fly-fishing trip*.

A dark sky closed in on the canyon, and the crowns of the redwoods began to sway. The first truly hard raindrops fell at a slant. Ferns dripped with glittery beads, and a steady drumming began on the forest canopy. The wind blew harder down the canyon; sheets of rain whipped out of the sky. The tops of the redwoods swayed hard in the gusting wind, shaking loose seed cones no bigger than olives. Bay laurels bent under the weight, their acorn-like fruits rattling down. Giant horsetails along the creeks fluttered and waved. Side streams bursting with rainwater emptied into the main channel.

The wind died away but the downpour continued, pounding the surface of the river to a froth. The great forest was saturated. Redwoods stood astride banks lost in smokelike mist and rain, their presence now felt more than seen. The river ran like café au lait.

We took shelter in a bar in Garberville, and Hal began downing tequila like it was California chardonnay. I think a drug deal was going down at the table next to us. This was the Emerald Coast, after all, the marijuana capital of California. Hal's voice rose as the level of the tequila in his glass dropped. He had a few strong things to say on the subject of effluvial geomorphology and bankside erosion, and he uttered dark oaths against the U.S.

Forest Service and its mascot, "Stumpy the Bear." Since the bar was probably full of laid-off mill hands, I figured it might be prudent for us to leave quietly. It was boom times in the woods, but tough times in the mills. Raw timber was being shipped directly for processing overseas; mills were opening in Mexico as quickly as they were closing in northern California. There was an argument over who would drive the pickup, and I won.

Hal had a friend up around Crescent City who would be letting us use his cabin, and we needed to get back on the highway. We fled the storm north toward Oregon, windshield wipers on high. Well past nightfall, we were safe inside a cabin close by the Oregon border, snug beneath sheltering redwoods. The woodstove glowed warmly, and we stared at it like a television set. Hal fine-tuned the flue and draft as if he were adjusting a pair of old-fashioned rabbit-ear antennas. He was padding around in his moist socks, his tequila high by now a hangover depression. He was wearing a sweatshirt given to him by his girlfriend; it said in lettering on the front: DE GUSTIBUS NON EST DISPUTANDUM.

Outside the rain closed in and seemed to take on the shape of the cabin. In the morning, weather permitting, we would be fishing the most beautiful steelhead river in California.

At Jedediah Smith Redwoods State Park, the morning sun was piercing the veil of ground mist left over from the storm's pageant.

Sunlight broke in a grove of ancient trees to illuminate a display of transforming wonder. Redwood trunks loomed before us that the night before had receded into the rain and fog. Broken sunlight spilled from a high canopy. Tan-and-cream mushrooms poked their capstools out of the permanent shade beside the redwood trunks. The shaggy fronds of sword ferns arched out of forest nooks between redwood burls and family rings, and maidenhair ferns overspilled stream banks and mossy seeps.

The wet duff that carpeted the forest floor muffled sounds to a worshipful hush. Trees rose hundreds of feet; they might have been alive at the time of Columbus, of Christ, or even the Buddha. Dramatizing their great height was the fact that their trunks were bare of branches for the first one or two hundred feet, so that when you stared up at them from the ground their shaggy crowns seemed to sweep the sky. I craned my neck, and the treetops appeared to lean in a sheltering circle above me. A redwood tree might fall in a storm or simply topple under its own immense weight. But mostly these trees seemed impervious to time. They were the tallest living things in creation, and some of the oldest, and I couldn't walk into a grove without thinking I was being admitted into one of nature's holiest sanctums.

A cold, fern-lined trail came out upon the jade-green Smith River. I had never seen a steelhead river so clean after a rain. Its startling green color came not only from the reflection of evergreens, but also from a mineral in the rocks called serpentine.

Moss and lichen embroidered the cliff face, and the steeply pitched boulders and rocky points jutted out over pristine pools. The black-green, shadowed depths reflected towering redwood trees and pillowing clouds. The water in the shallows was so clear you were tricked into believing it wasn't there at all.

The Smith nurtures the largest salmon and steelhead in California. It's the largest undammed river in the state and one of the cleanest waterways in America. It's so pure that it astonishes people who've forgotten what water is supposed to look like.

The air in the canyon felt magical, almost windless. An osprey banked, swinging easily above the misty spires, the jade river passing under its gaze. I could speak for an hour about the beauty of the Smith, but I had yet to catch a steelhead in it. I had gone a thousand casts without a strike.

At the run known as the White Horse Riffle, I mended my line, following its swing downcurrent. Light wavered on underwater river cobblestones. The fly turned on the current, swinging into the heart of a great mystery.

Hal fished in his usual state of heightened avidity. The river seemed to pour into his bloodshot, hungover eyes. Amazingly Hal's crisp casting showed few signs of a man who had mistaken tequila for table wine the night before.

A hundred yards or so of gorgeous water filled my eyes. A poet once said that we all have a core that is ecstatic. Each of us looks up in wonder; each of us experiences moments of eternity. This was mine. I had found early on that I had discovered my ecstatic core on trout rivers such as these.

I tied on a small green-and-black fly that seemed to match the tone of the emerald pool. The river slid by in a bright rush. We wove our casts into the air as clouds drifted across the redwood sky and driftboats glided into view.

Not far downstream another angler backed deliberately onto the gravel bar, his rod bent, his taut line angling far out into the deep run where a steelhead strained near the bottom, using the current to its best advantage. The man skillfully controlled his line, changing the direction of the bending rod tip to keep the struggling fish off balance. Ten minutes later he was pulling a bright steelhead onto the gravel.

In all, seven or eight fly casters worked the swift flow, but there was plenty of good yardage between us. Across the water, a few shore casters hurled terminal tackle into the deeper runs. Over the course of time, several fish were hooked and either landed or broken off. From time to time the peaceful canyon rang with ecstatic shouts and cries. One steelhead left the water in a silvery arc and burned line downstream so fast, the rest of us in the lineup had to reel in to let fish and angler pass. The man splashed in the shallows and scrambled wordlessly over the gravel stones, frantically trying to keep up.

Sometimes I would think I had a strike, only to find myself hung up on the bottom. The granite bedrock of the Smith River is notorious for its toothy snags. I pointed my rod toward the horizon and pulled, snapping off the fly. The most pathetic sight in fishing is someone forever trying to free himself from the bottom.

Somewhat discouraged, I sat down on the gravel bar to eat a sandwich and enjoy the beautiful canyon. Above the mossy cliffs, the giant redwood groves of the streamside flats yielded to a mixed understory of smaller redwoods, tan oaks, vine maples, shaggy ferns, and a wet tangle of ground cover. Unlike the deep hush in the monarch groves, the slope forest was full of flitting sounds, like that made by the winter wren, whose song fell on the air like a glass instrument.

A trail led from the gravel bar into the redwoods, and having climbed it, I found myself on a bluff overlooking a bend in the river, its pools emerald and radiant. The river curved clear out of sight, and in scattered spots a ragged mist drifted over the tree-tops. The driftboats below accented the canyon's grandeur. From my vantage point I watched a big fish jump and fall back in the river with a suctionlike splash, one that echoed off the granite walls. It was the sound I imagined my typewriter would make if I dropped it off the cliff into the river.

Staring down at the water, I could see the outline of a steelhead holding in a slick at the lower end of the pool. And another and another. I climbed down to the spot where a short, exposed gravel bar met the river. It was much deeper than it had appeared from above, and I couldn't get within casting range.

One of the things I discovered while steelhead fishing in northern California was that winter steelhead would not move very far to take a fly. They were not like the more energetic summer steelhead on the Umpqua. The cold slowed down their metabolism. They had to be fished with heavy sunken lines.

When winter rains began raising the levels of California streams, steelhead would head upstream, stopping to rest in holes formed by boulders and sharp bends; along the edges of heavy riffles; in the slicks that formed immediately above and below whitewater runs; and especially in the wide tailouts of pools. Not all of these lies could be reached with a fly rod, but the shallower tailouts and riffles certainly could.

Hal and I fished hard throughout the short winter day. Some of the pools were too deep, hopeless without a boat. Occasionally we would see a steelhead roll beyond the reach of our casts, and we envied the anglers in their driftboats.

Our pool began to sink into deep shadow as the sun set behind the wall of redwoods. The brittle air grew colder and the sky changed to the darker royal blue of a winter dusk.

"This is what we have instead of religion," said Hal, staring into the canyon's colorless light.

I would have been happy to hang it up. My arm was tired; my casting had become half hearted. Hal's turnovers were still full of authority and the boundless hope with which he'd started his day.

I felt a kind of suction bump on my fly, and when I raised the rod—expecting another snag—a steelhead vaulted skyward like voltage leaping a transformer. It was the surprise of my life. The steelhead—the biggest I had ever felt on the end of a line—sounded and rose again like an ICBM missile, out and out, water streaming off its silver back. It cartwheeled end over end and fell backward with a smack that jarred the pool. Spray flew everywhere with each shake of its powerful head.

The steelhead made an insane downriver run and leapt one more time, shaking itself along its entire length. My line snapped back, twining itself around the rod tip. Line and leader trailed limply downstream. It was all over forever.

"Way to go, Slick. You let the mother get away," said my friend Hal.

I felt enervated, and quickly tied on another fly. But I was shaking with cold and could almost feel the onset of hypothermia. The day had passed into the liquid mercury of evening. I knew it was time to go. The redwood trees were a dark presence on the opposite bank. Not least on my mind was the six-hour drive I still had to make back to San Francisco.

Back on the highway, sitting in the pickup, watching passing reflectors and the moon racing across the darkened tops of the redwoods, I thought about the steelhead that had broken my line, and how surely it would have been the biggest trout I had ever taken. I played the fight repeatedly over in my mind, until the sounds of the highway became the sounds of the river. I had seen the best that this sport has to offer. I had seen steelhead holding their own in the river, creatures of unshakable purpose. They had survived their journey and they had come home. They made me feel like cheering.